# The
# Blueprint
# to Happy

The Blueprint to Happy
Copyright © 2024 by Adam S. Peters
*All world rights reserved.*

No part of this book may be reproduced, stored in a retrieval system, or transmitted in any form or by any means electronic, mechanical, photocopying, recording or otherwise, without the prior consent of the publisher.

Readers are encouraged to go to www.MissionPointPress.com to contact the author, or to contact the publisher about how to buy this book in bulk at a discounted rate.

Contact the author via adam@mindmaprenovations.com.

MISSION POINT PRESS

Published by Mission Point Press
2554 Chandler Rd.
Traverse City, MI 49696
(231) 421-9513
www.MissionPointPress.com

Editing by Hart Cauchy
Book design by Sarah Meiers
Cover art by J Caleb Clark, jcalebdesign.com, 2023
Illustrations for figures 1, 4 and 5 by Summer Graziano

ISBN: 978-1-961302-46-4
Library of Congress Control Number: 2024905688

Printed in the United States of America

# THE BLUEPRINT TO HAPPY

Become a better problem solver, broaden and deepen your relationships, and heal faster with this highly accessible and effective six-step process.

**BY ADAM S. PETERS**

**MISSION POINT PRESS**

# TABLE OF CONTENTS

Foreword by Ada Takacs......................vii
A Love Letter to the Neurodivergent Reader............1
Introduction..................................5
Practical Applications........................14
What Kind of Happiness Are We Talking About?.........16
The Science: It's a Numbers Game ...................22
Establishing a Baseline ............................29
The Benefits, Part 1 ..............................33
The Process ....................................41
   Step 1: Declare Your Intent .......................47
   Step 2: (Train Yourself to) Notice...................55
   Step 3: Interrupt the Negative Pattern ..............64
   Step 4: Investigate ..............................70
   Step 5: Reframe -> Rewire,
     AKA Tell Yourself a Better Story ..................82
   Step 6: Repeat ..................................94
Best Practices ..................................96
Mantras and Maxims to Live By .....................124
The Blueprint and Weathering Adversity ..............134
The Benefits, Part 2 .............................140
Parting Words ..................................161
You're done reading! Now what?....................165
References .....................................167
About the Author ...............................170

# FOREWORD

*I beat Adam at leg wrestling* more than twenty years ago. He was shocked, which was kind of the point. We'd just had a discussion of what he would do if he were a passenger on a hijacked plane. Adam, after all, had already earned his first degree blackbelt in karate by then. That day I showed him what the element of surprise can do, because there are many surprises in life.

I knew this would only work once. You see, I had been leg wrestling for years and had a process that served me well. Despite multiple requests for a rematch, I knew not to leg wrestle my nephew again. I had known him his entire life. I knew he would have a process of his own within minutes after the loss, and it would be better than mine. As it turned out, this was the first lesson of many that we've shared with each other over the years.

Adam has come a long way from where he started. Back then, teenage Adam was going to school full time and working two jobs, often hidey holed in a dim, makeshift bedroom that once served as a back porch to his parents' home. While he had plenty of opportunities for socialization, he seemed disconnected from others, and maybe more importantly, disconnected from himself.

I could see this so clearly because I've met more people in my lifetime than most. My family travelled with the carnival for nearly a decade where I spent the long days of my youth on the midway interacting with literally hundreds, if not thousands, of people. As an adult, I worked in conservation (primarily forestry) where I taught outdoor education and later served as a leader in Incident Management. I spent summers in wildland fire camps across the United States and my winters coaching U.S. and Canadian teams through the Incident Command System, teaching topics like Stress First Aid and Team Dynamics. I'd say I have a pretty good understanding of how people react in emergency situations.

I find it interesting that adult Adam saw the Happy in me. What does a child carney have to be happy about? Or an adult who has chosen a lifetime of service to communities that have literally burned to the ground, sometimes losing their sons and daughters to the battle?

If there is a theme to all that I have witnessed in life, it is fundamental human resilience. I saw families, despite tough times, push money into my mother's hand while their children jumped up and down in anticipation of their three tickets to ride. Having responded to major wildland fires, I witnessed communities who suffered losses almost too extreme to bear join together to rebuild, often times stronger than before. Maybe I absorbed more of that resilience than I thought, and that was what Adam saw in me.

Years after our aunt/nephew leg wrestling match, Adam earned his 2nd degree blackbelt in karate, a demanding undertaking known for teaching self-regulation and discipline. This level of commitment, combined with his natural curiosity of human nature and increasing professional experience as a process expert, set the perfect conditions for the creation of The Blueprint to Happy. From the outside looking in, it might be surprising that

Adam could make his way from the disconnected teen I once knew to the Happiness Ambassador that he is today. But it is no surprise to me. I've had the honor of a front-row seat to the transformation and I'm a much better person because of it.

Before walking the path of the Blueprint with Adam, I would have told others that I had no need to assess my own happiness. Well, the element of surprise once again teaches the best lessons and I now realize the process has helped me in profound ways.

One example is when my friend asked if I was excited for my upcoming retirement party and my response was "I'll be glad when it's over." Later Adam asked why a positive and exciting event in my life (celebrating my retirement is a good thing) would bring such a negative response. That one question made me realize that I have always had a "I'll believe it when I see it" mindset.

Adam suggested instead of thinking in terms of "I have to" to simply change my words to "I get to" when referring to upcoming events. It wasn't very long before my entire outlook changed. I now find myself excited for the day to come instead of telling my brain I'm being forced to do something. It's like a veil has lifted. Words matter.

One of the many great things about The Blueprint to Happy is that it makes no assumptions of what Happy means to you. We are all different and so are our needs and desires. The Blueprint accommodates that.

I am forever grateful Adam could identify that I was happy and make the connections to give that to himself, and with the Blueprint, share his gift with others.

I attribute much of my happiness to a life partner who brings out the best in me and the friendships I've cultivated over the years. My happiness can also be directly linked to the time I spend outdoors. Afterall, Mother Earth makes no assumptions and passes no judgement. With that in mind, I'm always drawn to a good nature analogy.

I may have been the happy acorn that Adam stumbled across, but he planted the concept, watered the seedling, kept it well fed, exposed it to sunlight, studied how to make it prosper, and grew a majestic tree named Blueprint to Happy. I'm looking forward to watching the forest grow.

— Aunt Ada

# (1)
# A LOVE LETTER TO THE NEURODIVERGENT READER

*Before we dive in,* I would like to take a moment to speak to the wonderful and lovely neurodivergent people that rightfully wish to pursue happiness and are reading this book. Neurodivergent is a term used to describe individuals whose neurological development and functioning differ from the so-called neurotypical or typical population. Conditions like Autism Spectrum Disorder (ASD), Attention-Deficit/Hyperactivity Disorder (ADHD), and Dyslexia are considered neurodivergent. Beyond these conditions characterized by neurological differences, I consider personality disorders to fall into the category of neurodivergence, although that is not an official designation. Borderline, Narcissistic, Obsessive-Compulsive, and Avoidant are examples of personality disorders that I believe are at least in part driven by the difference in neurological structures when compared to those without disorders.

The Blueprint has shown promise with neurodivergent people who have applied the process and stuck with it. With that said, there may be more challenges for the neurodivergent reader to apply this process than there would be with a neurotypical reader. A neurodivergent reader may see the most improvement in their lives by combining the learnings of this book with other support mechanisms such as cognitive behavior therapy (CBT), dialectical behavior therapy (DBT), eye movement desensitization and reprocessing (EMDR) therapy, Internal Family Systems (IFS) — also known as "parts work" therapy — and/or certified life coaching. Medication for conditions like ADHD may also be the difference maker when it comes to successfully leveraging the Blueprint. Medication for depression may also be appropriate; there is no amount of work on mindset that can account for a chemical imbalance in the brain. You should consult with your primary care physician or a psychiatrist to explore medication options if you feel like medication would be an appropriate option for you.

Again, this doesn't mean that the Blueprint can't or won't work for you. Depending on your specific type of neurodivergence, there could be additional challenges (persistent intrusive thoughts, severe emotional dysregulation, troubles maintaining focus, etc.) that make executing these techniques difficult for you. And that's okay. One of my overarching goals in publishing this Blueprint is to give the neurotypical reader more ready access to the love, compassion, and grace that is already within all of us. My hypothesis is that this will result in more capability and eagerness to build communities and understanding for all kinds of people in this world — and that includes you.

Especially you, in fact. Because it is not as easy for you to change your thought patterns, it is incumbent on those who can to do so for the betterment of us all.

My hope and dream for helping others make space in their lives for the neurodivergent has very personal origins. I was estranged from my sister for over a decade, in large part because she is impacted by a mental health condition that is not very well understood by those who are not afflicted with it. From the outside looking in and without the capacity to broaden my mindset, her behaviors looked more like character flaws than a largely uncontrollable and disabling mental disorder. Furthermore, because I had not yet learned to have compassion for myself, it was impossible for me to have compassion for her. Due to the lack of support and awareness available to my sister, traumas deepened, and vital support was withheld.

It was only during my journey towards personal happiness that the compassion I began to feel for myself was able to spill over and broaden my mindset in a way that allowed me to genuinely show up for my sister.

If this book helps even one person do the same for their neurodivergent loved ones, I will consider it a tremendous success. Please know that I see you, I feel for you, and I love you.

Because trauma seems to be a significant contributor to personality disorders, I highly recommend the texts below that center around trauma healing. I invite you to check them out and see if they bring you closer to the eudaimonia which this book is dedicated to.

*What Happened to You* by Oprah Winfrey and Dr. Bruce Perry
*No Bad Parts* by Richard Schwartz
*The Body Keeps the Score* by Bessel Van Der Kolk

For those who may want to seek therapy, it can be helpful to know what kind of professionals are out there and what the difference is between them. Here is a short list that may help get you started:

- → **Psychologist** — Talk therapy like CBT or DBT
- → **Psychiatrist** — Professionals authorized to write prescriptions as needed for treatment in addition to talk therapy
- → **Social Worker** — Professionals who can assist you by connecting you with community resources
- → **LMFT** — Relationship therapy
- → **LPC** — Mental, behavioral, and emotional therapy

# (2)
# INTRODUCTION

*"I wish I could be more like you,"* I thought but did not say aloud. The "you" was my aunt Ada, who seemed to have mastered the art of being personable, resilient, and happy. On this occasion, I had been explaining to her how much I *lacked* personality, resilience, and happiness. I described it as a personal tragedy, beyond certain that changing my thoughts or behaviors would never change the outcomes in my life. The problem, I was sure, was everyone *else* — not me. I genuinely had no concept of what role I played in my very own life.

If that seems like a familiar mindset, this book was written for you.

Aunt Ada's advice to me that day was simple: decide to meet the moment with a positive word, and the rest will follow. As baffling as that was at the time, it makes perfect sense to me now after years of intentional self-discovery, study, and applied learnings. This book is a simple breakdown of the many resources and easily repeatable process-steps that helped me to achieve my own happiness. And yes, happiness is possible even in today's world. Even in times of great personal stress, uncertainty, and bad fortune.

My dream is that this book connects the dots for you in a way that is as accessible as it is meaningful. This Blueprint is a straight-forward, no frills process intended to give you all the guidance required for you to accomplish inner peace, confidence and, indeed, happiness — in whatever form that fits you and your unique life. As you transform your inner world to align with the Blueprint, you will find that you have become a better problem solver, that your relationships are deeper and broader than ever before, and the energy and good health of your body mirrors the strength of your positive outlook.

My relationship with my aunt has grown and deepened many times over since this brief exchange took place. Since then, I have learned about the many obstacles and disadvantages she had to overcome to become the person she is today. She was not, in fact, born personable, resilient, and happy — quite the opposite. For so many, the conditions in which we enter this world are not ideal, which is true even for those "born with it all." Regardless of our starting points in life, our biggest adversary can often be ourselves, held back by the instinct to focus our attention on the negatives in life. We compare ourselves to others, doom-scroll the news or social media, criticize ourselves and those around us, remain incurious, and neglect our own self-care.

However, the inverse is equally as true: our biggest *advocate* in life can also be ourselves. People who choose to be their own supporter, to love themselves and take care of their needs and act with kindness and positivity at the forefront of their minds are destined to flourish. Over time, I have learned that my own behaviors, thoughts, and mindsets — the emotional trajectory of my life — are perhaps the *only* things I have actual control over.

In other words, the only thing that had been holding me back was my belief that who I was and what I was capable of doing was out of my hands. By not questioning my beliefs, examining my thoughts, desires, and actions, or aspiring to be anything other than "default," I had made my life into a self-inflicted struggle.

I had all my basic needs met and then some — a good career with more opportunities readily available. A house with an affordable mortgage. A reliable car and all my bills met with money left over for savings — and to indulge in the occasional-to-frequent retail therapy session. And still, I was complaining about other people, my view of the world, and my place in it.

I wanted happiness but had no clue what it meant, and especially how to get it. Looking back on that conversation I realize that it was one of the first seeds in a garden that is still growing as I type — the fruit of which has matured and grown plentiful enough to share. My hope is that by sharing this metaphorical fruit through these pages, it will nourish your mind and spirit in a way that makes you more capable of being the architect of your own happiness.

## THE CURRENT SITUATION

Happiness is so important to the American psyche that it headlined the Declaration of Independence in 1776. Two hundred forty-seven years later and despite immense national wealth generation, the United States of America is one of the sickest and most poverty-stricken countries of the world's developed nations. We have the most mass shootings, lead the world in prison populations, and are 3rd in global suicide rates.[1]

How did one young nation's pursuit of happiness go so wrong? You may have an answer poised at the tip of your tongue — perhaps you are thinking it is because of corruption and money in politics,

---

[1] Our World in Data: Suicides https://ourworldindata.org/suicide

greed, rugged-individualism, or exploitation. These are real factors, and they are absolutely contributing to our current unhappy state.

However, I propose to you that they are only *symptoms* of the true root cause. That root cause is self-neglect on an individual level — neglecting the search for true happiness. Many people seek happiness in ways it can never be attained, looking outward rather than inward, often resulting in the belittlement of others in favor of their own gains or utter depression when happiness cannot be attained through external sources.

Society is a collection of individuals, and how we take care of ourselves and what we prioritize in our individual lives has a distinct and meaningful impact on the whole of our society. In this way, the health of society can be determined by the individual experience. Many people have given up on the pursuit of happiness and succumbed to the kinetic forces that have gotten us to this point. And so the majority rules — and the majority of individuals are unhappy.

I know because, as mentioned, I used to be one of these people. Cynical and certain that nothing could possibly make a difference while also secretly wishing that "someone" would "do something" about the dysfunction in our society.

And then I realized … I am "someone." I began to wonder what my role could and should be in helping to make the world a better place. This led me down the path that brought me to writing this book, and I am thrilled beyond belief that you are reading it. Because the truth is there *is* something you can do to help make the world a better place — you can make *your* world a better place.

In looking for ways to make a meaningful contribution to society, I realized that I had to start with myself, first. This is the most successful path to follow because the only thing any of us have actual control over is ourselves. And when enough people make the effort to do for themselves exactly what is outlined in this book, a tipping point will come, and we will all benefit as a result — even the folks who cannot or will not take the steps to improve their lives.

More on that later. For now, sit back, settle in, and join me on this life-changing journey.

## THE TURNING POINT

So, what happened? How did I get from unhappy to happy? As improbable as it seems, my path to happiness accelerated around the same time as a deadly global pandemic.

When March 2020 came, I was six months into what I had expected to be my dream job as a process expert at a global consultancy company. I was heads-down, intent on making a good impression by working long hours and agreeing to any and all assignments that came my way. I imagined myself excelling at warp speed and climbing the corporate ladder in no time flat. I was barely at home thanks to a long commute that had more to do with traffic than actual distance. The hobbies I enjoyed like volleyball, cycling, writing, and cooking were falling steadily to the wayside. I threw my whole self into my work identity, investing not only my time, but my emotional wellbeing into the oftentimes capricious environments that make up the landscape of corporate America.

This, I have come to realize, was my way — my choice — and how I conducted myself in work situations regardless of my employer. It often resulted in a steaming pile of unhappiness as I struggled to control things that were impossibly outside of my sphere of influence, let alone control. When my efforts went unrecognized, unappreciated, or were even resented, my sleep suffered, and anger was always close to the surface. I often reacted by doubling down on my already not-so-great approach, working myself up even more when that somehow did not magically produce better results.

But in late February when the first confirmed case of COVID-19 was announced in the very county in which I commuted to work, something started to shift. I had, after all, seen the movie *Contagion* (2011) about a highly contagious and fatal virus spread via respiratory droplets. I understood what the words "exponential" and "deadly" meant, which the various media outlets were beginning to use more and more in combination with COVID-19.

That week, I had a frank conversation with one of the members of the Risk Assessment team our company had put together in response to the COVID threat. Their task was to determine what our giant company should do given that the novel disease was already keeping cruise ships from docking at ports for fear of further outbreaks. I pointed out the obvious: the disastrous repercussions of a workforce our size being hit with mass illness all at once. The mad scramble to send everyone to work from home came just a short week or two after that conversation.

It can be easy to forget how little we knew back then about COVID-19. How much the news was filled with speculation, uncertainty, and new, exciting technical glitches because news anchors and talk show hosts had been sent home to do their work, too. I can still recall the reticence on the faces of government officials as they admitted that a *best-case* scenario for the US now that the disease had escaped containment was 100,000–200,000 total deaths. As of the writing of this book, the US death toll from COVID-19 stands at over 1.1 million, which many experts agree is probably an undercount.

It was in those first months during what I considered to be "COVID Jail," that I sat down and asked myself THE question:

"If I died tomorrow," which now seemed more a possibility

than it had ever been before that time, "would I be happy with how I lived my life?"

The answer was a clear and resounding, "**No.**"

The main drivers? I was overweight, under stimulated, easily emotionally triggered, and disconnected from both my friends and my family. And not because of COVID — all of this I had done on my own. It took a worldwide pandemic for me to make an accurate inventory of how I was living my life. I realized that I didn't *live* in the home I had bought eight years prior — I just *stayed* there. Nothing was optimized for regular use, from the pots and pans in my kitchen to the back yard, which was little more than a dirt patch with some uneven pavers.

It was akin to a near death experience — at 34 years old. For all the havoc it has wreaked on the world, COVID gave me the time and the space to genuinely reevaluate myself, the world, and my place in it. It began my journey of writing this book, and perhaps because of my process background, allowed me to navigate the path towards happiness in a way I can now see as systematic, and thus capable of being shared with what I hope are similar results for you.

Little by little, I used this process to address all the things that contributed to my feelings of negativity — starting with working out in the back yard, then home improvements. I started calling my parents and friends more. I picked back up some unfinished books, which went on to inspire me to formally upskill myself through affordable programs I could attend on nights and weekends in areas that would not only help me, but eventually help me help others.

Those skills empowered me to set better boundaries for my work-life balance, in both the time and emotional investments I made. That, in a surprising but welcome twist of events, made me a much better coworker and employee with literally zero changes to my job, pay, or responsibilities.

With work better managed than ever, I challenged myself to outline the details of how it was possible to make such incredible progress towards improving my life. This led to the construction of a one-on-one program designed to replicate the results I experienced. Not only did the program confirm that these techniques work in an empirical and measurable way, but I also had the pleasure of witnessing the incredible transformations of others firsthand. Changes in mood and confidence were evident to me even before my clients noticed the changes.

All the improvements in the quality of my and others' surroundings, mental wellbeing, and life in general were made possible by this Blueprint. The next logical step seemed to be to get it into the hands of as many people as possible, and what better way to do that than to write a book that can be personalized and kept handy for years to come?

In conducting the research for this book and my studies in general, I have come to realize that there are many published works that outline the possible paths to happiness quite well. Many authors, experts, sages, and master practitioners have urged people towards happiness since antiquity as evidenced by the wisdom of the ancient Greeks and even further back through texts like the Hindu Bhagavad Gita.

So why add another book to the heap?

Well, you're reading this one, and if nothing has helped you yet, this might. And happiness, my friend, is worth it. This Blueprint prioritizes explaining the *how*, rather than the why. Why we are unhappy is different for everyone, and I think we can all agree that unhappiness is rampant — I don't need to prove that point.

Instead, this book offers you a practical and accessible way to materially improve your life, full stop.

The Blueprint also has the advantage of being written at a time where our understanding of neuroscience is at an all-time high, allowing us to consciously work in collaboration with our brains like never before. We know that all people learn and internalize differently; each mind map is unique in its composition and how it was created. We need a variety of voices sharing these learnings and experiences in order to resonate with the maximum number of people.

Most of this book is intended to benefit the reader at the individual level, however you should know up front that it is my ultimate goal to recruit you into something that I call the Community Happiness Project, where participation is mandatory. The single ask of the Community Happiness Project is that you inject as much positivity into your life as possible and find ways to share positivity with your community. My hope is that by creating enough positive mindsets at an individual level, we can go on to make the world a better, more creative, caring, healthy, and giving place. More on that in the Benefits, Part 2 chapter.

This is the Blueprint to Happy: a process that anyone can follow to broaden their minds and live their best possible life, no matter what the circumstances. It doesn't cost money (other than what you might have spent on this book), and it doesn't require any more time and energy than you are already using in your day. In fact, should you master this process, you may find yourself expending a lot less energy than you used to, saving it to spend on the really good stuff in life.

Is this your turning point? Let's find out.

# (3)
# PRACTICAL APPLICATIONS

**There are 12** Practical Application exercises in the Blueprint which are intended to help you get the most out of the process and increase your chances of successfully building a long-term preference for positivity. You will recognize these exercises by looking for this icon:

You are invited to take notes and respond to the Practical Application exercises right here within the book.

If you would like more space to write, are reading on a digital format, or listening to the audiobook, you can find a free downloadable, editable, and printable workbook at www.blueprinttohappy.com. Readers can also use the QR code below to access The Blueprint to Happy Official Workbook:

## (4)
# WHAT KIND OF HAPPINESS ARE WE TALKING ABOUT?

*The ancient Greeks* had two words for happiness. The first is the origin of the word "hedonism" — it describes the kind of happiness that you feel from an experience, connection, or sensation. Everything from a delicious meal to really great sex falls under the ancient Greek category of "hedonia." This kind of happiness is temporary and prone to turn into agony if you take it too far. The torturous chocolate cake scene from *Matilda* comes to mind, where the evil Misses Trunchbull makes a student eat an enormous chocolate cake as punishment for allegedly eating a single slice of hers.

Hedonia is as easy to summon as a food delivery via your phone or a quick trip to one of the numerous liquor stores in your town. This temporary happiness feeds into the delusion that happiness can be achieved through external means — that it's entirely transactional in nature.

The second kind of ancient Greek happiness is called

"Eudaimonia," and is the kind of happiness you experience when you are living in accordance with your higher calling, or highest potential. This is a lasting happiness, one that can be sustained for long periods of time and permeates every aspect of your life. It is the kind of happiness that underlies the healthiest kind of resiliency, has been proven to help you live longer,[2] and gives you the kind of perspective that makes it easy to see the vast number of options that are available to you at any time.

Happiness has also been described as separation from suffering. Suffering, in the context of this Blueprint, is akin to negative thoughts — the insidious kind of suffering we inflict on ourselves with the same ease as breathing. As Dalai Lama Haruki Murakami once said so eloquently: "Pain is inevitable. Suffering is optional."

*Eudaimonia* is the kind of happiness this book offers a Blueprint to.

In order to get to eudaimonia — where one realizes their fullest potential — one must set the conditions for doing so. The process offered in later chapters of this book does exactly that: help you set the conditions to live up to your fullest potential. The truth is that I do not know what that means for you. Happiness looks different for everyone. For some, happiness might be a quiet existence surrounded by close family and friends, supporting them in their goals and ambitions. For others it might be excelling at the top of their field without the risk of burnout or neglecting other key areas of their lives. Everyone's drives and passions are different, which

---

[2] Danner, D.D., D.A. Snowdon and W.V. Friesen (2001), "Positive emotions in early life and longevity: Findings from the nun study." B.R., M.D. Slade, et al. (2002), "Longevity increased by positive self-perceptions of aging," *Journal of Personality and Social Psychology* 83: 261-70; and Ostir, G.V., K.S. Markides, et al (2000), "Emotional wellbeing predicts subsequent functional independence and survival," *Journal of the American Geriatrics Society* 48:473-78

is one of the marvelous things about coexisting on this planet together; we all have the chance to forge our unique path based on the internal compass that guides our attention and aspirations. We all benefit when diverse passions are pursued, as no one person can be all things. The collective potential of individuals is where our strength truly lies.

Keeping the uniqueness of happiness in mind, I believe there is a universal and enabling truth at the center of achieving happiness: it must begin with casting off negative thought *patterns*.

Note that I do not say the eradication of negative thoughts; negative thoughts can be both useful and necessary. They can get us out of unsafe or unpleasant situations. When leveraged in healthy ways, negative thoughts rightly narrow our focus so we can act quickly and efficiently in response to circumstances ranging from inconvenient to dire.

> **"If suffering is avoidable, the meaningful thing to do is to remove its cause, for unnecessary suffering is masochistic rather than heroic. If, on the other hand, one cannot change a situation that causes his suffering, he can still choose his attitude."**
> — Viktor Frankl

It is far more important to shift the *pattern* of your thoughts. Your brain loves patterns and loves shortcuts even more. Your brain makes no judgement on the patterns you have naturally established. If you have a predominately negative thought pattern, your brain is happy to utilize those connections effectively and efficiently until the day you die. Your brain does not care that the possibilities in your life have been narrowed because of this, and the mystery as to why you never seem to have energy or access to the creativity you once had will remain a mystery. Your brain cares the most about what it is *used to* doing, and it will defend those familiar patterns with surprising ferocity.

The good news is that you are here now, taking in these words and thoughts. So, one mystery has been solved, and now the work can begin.

And yes, it is work. But because your brain loves shortcuts, it's the kind of work that gets easier over time. The time it takes to change negative thought patterns into positive ones pays off at the tipping point. As you will read in the next chapter, when it comes to the brain (just like society), the majority rules.

Your job, and the focus of this Blueprint, is to shift the balance of your thoughts enough to transform a predominately negative mindset into a predominately positive mindset.

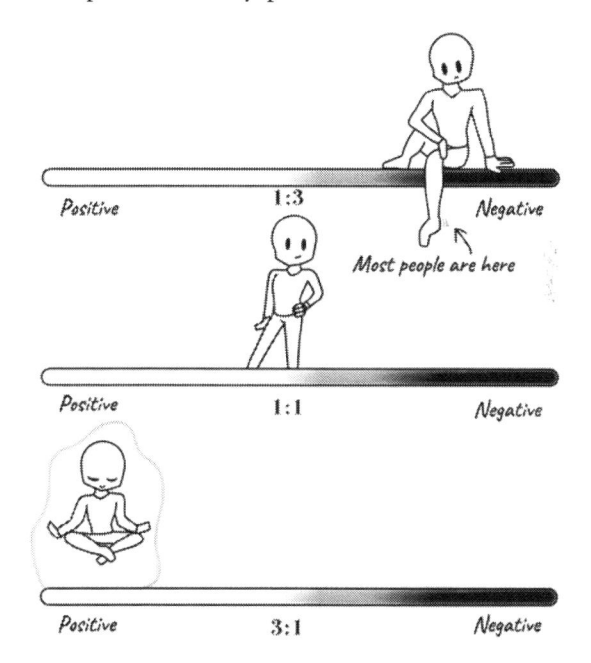

Figure 1

When this is accomplished, there is very little that can hold you back. This is because viewing the world from a place of positivity allows you to be a better problem solver, avoid the health risks associated with stress, and recover much faster from hardships. At an individual level the implications are wonderful. At a cumulative level, the implications are *astounding*.

**PRACTICAL APPLICATION #1**

Take a few minutes to jot down some of your thoughts on what living in alignment with your highest potential or purpose might look like. What would you do if you had more time, energy, and mental resources to do it? What is your soul drawn to do that is not related to physical gratification, where you feel deeply connected and fulfilled even when there is no monetary or outside incentive?

# (5)

# THE SCIENCE: IT'S A NUMBERS GAME

*In her 2009 publication* Positivity, Professor Barbara Fredrickson — a pioneer in the field of positive emotions — explains that positivity (although she explicitly does not call it happiness) is what allows humans to "broaden and build." Broaden as in our mindsets and build as in make things real in this world that were not real before.

She explains it like this: humans for a long time were nomadic, handling the dangers in their lives by not staying in one place for too long. However, at some point the idea to fortify themselves came to be. The most lasting and successful of all fortifications, things like great city walls and castles, could not be accomplished quickly. Oftentimes they took generations to build. But the decision to make the effort is an acknowledgement of the future safety that would be achieved. It was a broader perspective that allowed us to collectively level up, as it were. Professor Fredrickson proposes that the ability to take this broad perspective is the result of positive emotions rather than negative ones.

Professor Fredrickson suggests — and has the science to back it up — that negative emotions narrow our focus and keep us stuck, whereas positive emotions broaden our focus and allow us to see many more possibilities available to us. Thus, the evolutionary justification for positive emotions has been established. Castles, in other words, were acknowledgements to the benefits of safety, which allows us to continue to have positive thoughts so we may achieve more, which we most certainly have.

Our capacity for positive thoughts has turned into a superpower that has distinguished human beings in a meaningful way. It is a superpower that we have, despite our many achievements, only scratched the surface of.

Claims have been made that, on average, 80% of our thoughts are negative. And of those 80%, 95% are repeated negative thoughts. These figures are frequently associated with a study conducted by the National Science Foundation, although the primary source for this claim remains elusive. However, if true, this would leave only 20% for positive and neutral thoughts. Pause for a moment to consider if this feels like it could be true for you.

80% Negative Thoughts

95% of all negative thoughts are repeats

20% Positive or Neutral Thoughts

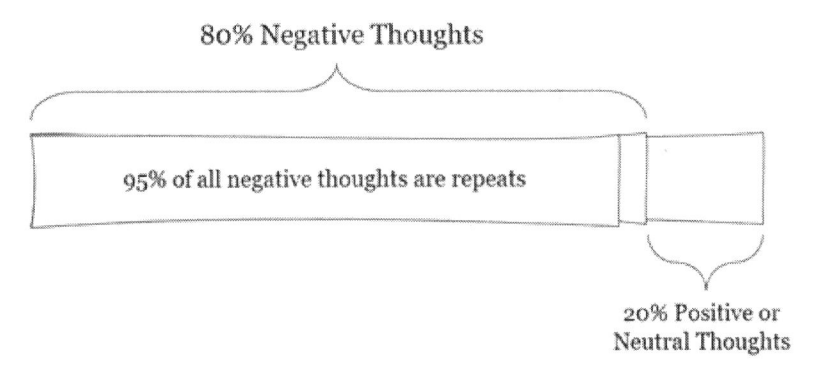

Figure 2

Professor Fredrickson's research has shown that of all her study participants, only about 25% of people have a positive to negative thought ratio sufficient to be considered "flourishing" in life. That to me indicates that most people do, in fact, have majority negative thought patterns which restrict their ability to live their best lives.

Because of the continued advancements of neuroscience, we have a much better idea of how our neural networks are formed and reinforced. The idea of a "majority rules" when it comes to negative and positive thoughts seems credible when taken against the understanding of the mechanics of our brains. Neurons have two ends, one for transmitting and one for receiving, connected by an insulated tube-like structure called an axon. Think about two cups connected by a string where one person speaks with the cup to their mouth and the other listens with the cup to their ear. Only in this case, each cup can grow multiple transmission and receiving points and transfer information at the speed of light. You have approximately *a hundred billion* of these neurons, and each one has multiple connectors that form a network used to process inputs, respond, and make decisions.

Figure 3

On each end of the neuron, multiple transmitting and receiving connectors are formed or reduced depending on the brain's needs. If we continue to learn and make connections, the neurons continue to generate connectors so we can make even more associations. As far as we know, there are no limits to how many connections can be made.

The connections we use the most are solidified and become the preference for how we think. The connections we use the least eventually shrink and disappear entirely if lack of use persists. This is how your brain forms shortcuts for thinking. Thought patterns. Ways of thinking that can be reused and applied to any number of situations as a default. Patterns that are regularly used are like superhighways, allowing your thoughts and reactions to execute quickly with little effort. Patterns less used are more like walking paths — and if you want to widen them, you must take the path more often until it grows to the size of a superhighway.

The term "neuroplasticity" refers to the ability of neurons to add or remove connections, as well as to repurpose existing connections. Neuroplasticity is another superpower that every human on earth has at their disposal, a quality that has become even more powerful because we are now aware of our abilities to change our thinking. Neuroplasticity is what gives us the ability to rewire our brains; this is something that happens organically already, but with conscious effort we can be the architects of our own mind-maps. We can be the architects of our own happiness.

So, if you are a person who has negative patterns dominating 80% of your thoughts on any given day, great news! Neuroplasticity is your way out. The opportunity for you to improve the quality of your life — to achieve that sweet, sweet eudaimonia — is a very exciting prospect. Because not only is it possible to do, you are also holding the Blueprint in your hand that explains exactly how to do it.

As mentioned, I am far from the first person to write on the topic of happiness or positivity. These concepts almost certainly predate the ancient Greeks from which we get the needed nuance to begin this conversation. I have drawn from many great contemporary minds during my own journey towards eudaimonia, a couple of them already mentioned and the rest will be available in the References section at the end of this book. What I have noticed is that genuinely great advice offered as pathways to a better life (take up meditation, engage in gratitude exercises) seem to skip a vital step that allows for those practices to be truly meaningful.

That vital step is the everyday opportunity to shift negative thought patterns into positive ones. Once this is achieved, things like meditation, connecting with others, giving grace, mindfulness, and creative thinking will flow to and through you as easily as water flows downhill.

In short, training your brain to prefer positivity is simply a numbers game thanks to the nature of neuroplasticity. If you have 1,000 thoughts a day and 800 of them sound something like, "That driver is a real a-hole." "I hate my job." "That house is ugly." "This food is too salty." "My mother-in-law talks too much." "My kids won't leave me alone for two seconds." "My son never calls me." etc., then your brain has developed a preference for negativity, resulting in a narrowed world view, limited problem-solving abilities, and stress-related health conditions like hypertension, headaches, and heartburn.

With this Blueprint, those thoughts will sound more like, "That driver must be having a really hard day." "I wonder what I can do to make my job better?" "Next time I'll make my own food so it tastes how I like it." "That house could use some love." "My mother-in-law must really feel comfortable with me." "I'm so grateful for the time I have with my kids when they are young." And, "I'm going to let my son know how much I enjoy our talks, even if they don't happen as much as I'd like."

If you have 1,000 thoughts a day, you have 1,000 daily opportunities to tell yourself a better story, and in doing so, train your brain to prefer positivity. If you have 1,000 thoughts a day, you need only 501 of them to be positive to begin building your positivity preference. And just think, if 95% of our negative thoughts are a series of repeated thoughts, discovering what these are and making a mindful effort to change only a few of them around presents an amazing opportunity to improve your positive to negative thought ratios.

When in doubt, just remember: it's a numbers game. Majority rules!

**PRACTICAL APPLICATION #2**

Take a moment to jot down what your repeated negative thoughts tend to be. Identifying these thoughts now will accelerate your success with the Blueprint as you learn more about the process and begin to apply the steps to your life.

## (6)

# ESTABLISHING A BASELINE

*Anytime you are embarking* on an improvement effort, it will help to record a baseline so that you can look back and compare where you are three or six months down the road to where you started. The before and after picture of a home renovation, if you will — and who doesn't love those?

As a bonus, this step will give you additional insights into which emotions will be helpful to pay attention to as you work through the Blueprint process.

### PRACTICAL APPLICATION #3

To that end, I'm going to ask you to pick up your phone, or leverage your virtual assistant of choice (Alexa, Siri, Google Home, etc.), to put a reminder three and six months from now that will prompt you to return to these pages. Once you do that, come back and follow these steps:

1. Review the lists in both of the following tables — one is a Negative Emotion Inventory, and the other is a Positive Emotion Inventory.
2. If this is your first read, put a mark in the "Baseline" column next to any of the emotions you find yourself experiencing frequently (three to four times a week or more).
3. At the prompting of your three months reminder, do the same in the "Three Months Post-Read" column.
4. At the prompting of your six months reminder, do the same in the "Six Months Post-Read" column.

If the process is working for you, at three months you should start to notice less marks on the Negative Emotion Inventory table, and more marks on the Positive Emotion inventory table. By six months, the shift should be even more noticeable.

If this is not the case, use the comparison as an opportunity to examine how you are leveraging the Blueprint and if you need to try a different approach, experiment with new tools, or re-visit some of these chapters.

| Negative Emotion Inventory | Baseline | 3 Months Post-Read | 6 Months Post-Read |
|---|---|---|---|
| Aggression | | | |
| Anger | | | |
| Annoyance | | | |
| Anxiety | | | |
| Bitter | | | |
| Fearful | | | |
| Frustration | | | |
| Impatience | | | |
| Indifference | | | |
| Inferior | | | |
| Insecure | | | |
| Irritation | | | |
| Numb | | | |
| Rage | | | |
| Rejected | | | |
| Sad | | | |
| Scared | | | |
| Sleepy | | | |
| Withdrawn | | | |
| Worthless | | | |

| Positive Emotion Inventory | Baseline | 3 Months Post-Read | 6 Months Post-Read |
|---|---|---|---|
| Accepted | | | |
| Amused | | | |
| Confident | | | |
| Content | | | |
| Courageous | | | |
| Creative | | | |
| Curious | | | |
| Grateful | | | |
| Hopeful | | | |
| Inspired | | | |
| Interested | | | |
| Joyful | | | |
| Loving | | | |
| Optimistic | | | |
| Peaceful | | | |
| Playful | | | |
| Proud | | | |
| Successful | | | |
| Trusting | | | |
| Valued | | | |

# (7)

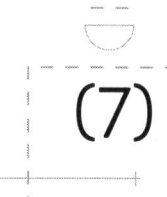

# THE BENEFITS, PART 1

*Change is challenging.* The intent of this chapter is not to incentivize you to be happy — no one needs to be sold on that. The intent of this chapter is to galvanize your commitment to the work of retraining your brain to prefer positivity. The low, discouraging moments that visit you on this journey may be tempting to give into. Familiar, even. You might decide not trying is the safest way to proceed, because if you don't try, you can't fail.

You, my friend, are worth the effort — so let this chapter be a reminder and motivation for you to stay true to the process and give you something pleasant to think about instead of succumbing to self-doubt.

## BETTER PROBLEM-SOLVING ABILITIES

Allow me to start with my personal favorite benefit of training your brain to prefer positivity: better problem-solving abilities. The reason this is so important is because there are real problems in the world — personal, familial, communal, national, global — and they do, in fact, need solving. On a personal level, much of what creates suffering in our lives will benefit from a keener eye and broader imagination to devise solutions that separate yourself from suffering. Your brain does its best work when it is at ease and feels safe, not overcome by strong emotions or anxieties. Following the Blueprint to Happy will allow you to get yourself to that place at will; with time it will become your default. The result is greater clarity with which you can take everything you know about your situation — the stresses, what resources are available to you, any previously failed attempts, etc. — and use that to calmly and confidently make a plan to improve your life.

I have always prided myself on being a good problem solver, even before the Blueprint. The trouble was, I was only great at solving *other people's problems*, and not my own. This is because I was emotionally attached to my problems, easily triggered, and incurious about my part to play in my own suffering. The Blueprint was what gave me the tools to solve the most important problems in my life – my own!

## MORE FRIENDS, CLOSE RELATIONSHIPS, AND RESOURCES TO HELP YOU

When you adopt positive thought patterns, your radiant charge will attract similar energies. So not only will you have more friends, but you will also have quality friends who want to help you accomplish your goals. When you cut out all the noise in your life that ultimately doesn't matter to you, you find out how much time you have to be present in your current relationships. If you are like me, this deepens relationships in ways you may have never considered possible. Making friends will also be easier, because you will have cultivated a sense of security in yourself that translates into confidence when interacting with others.

The empathy that is generated for yourself through the Blueprint will eventually flow so plentifully that extending empathy to others will become effortless. When you approach your relationships with empathy instead of comparison, resentment, or obligation, the depth to which they can expand will astonish you. The Blueprint helps you put feelings of pettiness and insecurity on the sideline indefinitely, and these are often the hurtles we face when making deep connections.

With more meaningful relationships in your life, you will also find that you have more resources at your disposal. After all, a single person can only know and do so much; by increasing your network of people who care about you and vice versa, your ability to knowledge-share, skill-trade, and engage in mutual support will be much greater. Community support, for example, has been shown to be one of the fastest pathways to trauma healing, and being a part of a community provides a sense of belonging and security that your mind naturally craves. Your brain will reward you by taking better care of your body, as described in the proceeding "Better health" segment.

The ways in which I have seen my relationships broaden and deepen with the help of the Blueprint continue to amaze me. Relationships with my immediate family deepened after years of only the shallowest of roots. Many of my long-standing triggers were identified with the help of the Blueprint, so I was able to stop the emotional domino effect that often held my familial relationships back. My preference for focusing on the positive allowed me to see the best in people instead of the worst. The extent to which this allowed me to broaden my view is incredible. My relationships are broader because I am far less likely to make snap negative judgements about new people in my life. I can meet the moment with curiosity and positivity. What I learned in this process is just how much I was closing myself off to the possibility of new connections because of my default preference to see and assume the negative in all situations.

My new positive worldview became evident from the outside looking in, and the number of people commenting on my ability to remain resilient with a sunny attitude grew over time. Amongst my growing friend group, I am known for spinning positive narratives around whatever the topic of conversation happens to be. I have become an uplifting force in my relationship network, strengthening the web and securing lasting and meaningful connections.

## BETTER HEALTH

The simple act of living creates daily microscopic and sometimes not-so-microscopic damage to your body, which is why your body has self-healing capabilities. The healing process is orchestrated by the subconscious which sends signals to the organs, nervous system, and even the bones in your body to perform various healing and immune-system functions. This process is most active at night when you are sleeping, when your mind can give full focus to the healing process. However, if you have poor sleep quality, or carry your waking anxiety into your evening, your brain's ability to orchestrate the healing process is greatly diminished.

Think of your body for a moment like a battleship. When not engaged in active battle, the crew is often hard at work performing routine maintenance, making improvements, and in general preparing itself for action. In the heat of battle, damage that occurs can only be mitigated; it is not until the ship is far away from danger that the major repairs will begin.

The same is true for your body. Your brain, so long as it believes it is in danger, will hold off on healing activities in favor of remaining vigilant for more danger. The difference between a battleship and your brain is that your brain is capable of believing there is danger when there is none. These are the negative thought patterns that force your mind into a state of hypervigilance, always on the lookout for more negativity to guard against.

Negative thought patterns prevent the active and comprehensive healing of your body in both waking and sleeping periods. Because it's a numbers game, the dominant patterns that keep you company all day continue into the night, resulting in anxiety dreams or even nightmares. Your body's inability to heal adequately can lead to disease or cell mutations that can lead to serious illness.

Positive thought patterns generate a sense of safety and rest, allowing your mind the space and security needed to initiate the healing process, day *and* night. Giving your body more time to heal results in better overall health, a longer life, and greater mental capacity to pursue even more improvements in your life.

A final note I will add on the topic of health is how positive thought patterns tend to keep you in the present moment more than negative ones. If you're experiencing a negative pattern, chances are you're reliving some kind of trauma or slight from the past, or anxiously worrying about the future. Positivity allows us to enjoy the moment as it exists in the present, and there is science behind why this provides health benefits. Your DNA is held together by endcaps called telomeres. When you are young, your telomeres are long, but as they duplicate with age, they shorten. Eventually, your telomeres disappear entirely and the DNA they hold together dies. When too many cells die, you become sick and at a certain tipping point telomere loss is fatal.

Scientists have studied the effects of mindfulness on telomeres and have found that mindfulness practices which require practitioners to be present in the moment *lengthen* telomeres in an observable way.[3]

## PEACE OF MIND

Finally, what building a preference of positivity can do for us is to bring ourselves a peace of mind about both the past and the future. Because we are hard-wired for negativity bias as a way of ensuring our survival, we tend to give more emphasis to the negative things that happen to us regardless of their overall significance or even how many good things happened around the same time. Before training my brain to prefer positivity, there was very little about my childhood that I cherished. For the most part, I didn't think about it at all, preferring to avoid the bad feelings altogether. This was akin to severing part of me from the whole. I had no idea how much of a gap or emptiness it left me with until I could look back on my childhood and pick out the things that brought me happiness and joy — of which there were many.

Being able to incorporate my childhood back into my identity had surprising benefits that are difficult to describe until you experience it yourself. It created a continuity in my life that allowed me to feel more authentic, as if before I had been hiding part of myself away, because that is exactly what I had been doing.

The past is over, but when we ruminate on the bad things that have happened to us, or deny the past altogether, we are creating suffering in the present. We all have the choice of what to focus our attention on, so why not focus on the positives and make peace with the past?

Similarly, when we develop a preference for positivity, the

---

[3] Zen meditation, Length of Telomeres, and the Role of Experiential Avoidance and Compassion, Published online 2016 Feb 22, https://www.ncbi.nlm.nih.gov/pmc/articles/PMC4859856/

future is a place of opportunity and advancement rather than potential doom and ruin. We get back all the processing power we were using to fret about things we cannot control, and instead settle into the optimism that whatever life decides to throw at us, we will make the best of it. Think about how much more pleasant your life will be when you shed the rumination of the past and your anxiety about the future. Not only will you achieve a higher level of peace, the positive feedback loop of creating a sense of stability and safety will make you more capable of weathering adversity and bouncing back from the inevitable hardships that come our way.

**PRACTICAL APPLICATION #4**

Take a few minutes to jot down what benefits you are looking forward to the most, or what you hope to get out of reading this book.

# (8)
# THE PROCESS

*I have always found* a certain amount of comfort in process. A process is a road map you can follow to get to a desired destination, or a blueprint to build something spectacular. A process will tell you what order to do things in and provides a clear-cut understanding about what outcomes you should expect at each step. A process implies some level of efficacy, that someone has walked these steps before and that they worked well enough to put onto paper. And the same is true with this process — I have walked these steps and I can say with great certainty and confidence that they work.

There are shared themes among the many sages and philosophers who have attempted to shepherd people into the promised land of happiness. One of the most common is the practice of meditation, which is a wonderful and effective way to encourage positive thoughts and feelings; however, deep meditation is not always practical as an entry-level step for the modern person who is already strapped for time and focus. It is for this reason I am proposing another approach. Every day, every *minute*, is an opportunity to make a tangible difference in our ability to be happy.

Every thought is an opportunity to make a deliberate choice about how we want to live our lives. And if you miss an opportunity, don't worry! The universe will happily serve you up another, and another, until your time here is done.

This process gives you endless chances to make the necessary pivots to shift negative thought patterns into positive ones. Once you have mastered the process, you may find yourself much more capable and eager to practice things like meditation and self-care.

Thanks to the mechanics of how our brains work, processes tend to get better, more efficient, and stronger the more that we use them. Just like riding a bike, there is a lot of upfront investment in learning how to begin, and then repetition to get better, followed by full mastery. This is called procedural memory, and once established it can be activated without conscious awareness or effort. In this way, the Blueprint to Happy starts as an exercise in discipline and persistence but is quickly automated. Discipline and persistence are innate in humans; we could not be where we are today without these qualities in significant quantities.

In fact, with enough consistency and persistence, humans can easily change the meaning of words. There is no specific reason why a fork is called a fork instead of a spoon, for example. Language is assigning sounds to describe objects — when learning a new language, the objects stay the same but our words for them will change. Our brains easily assimilate new names for objects with enough repetition and belief.

I will be asking you to deploy the same kind of discipline and persistence to this process, with the promise that once you cross the tipping point from negative to positive, the effort will become effortless and self-reinforcing within your procedural memory. The benefits outlined in the previous chapter will be yours for the taking.

That said, it may take some time to put these into consistent practice, and that's okay. I encourage you to practice these steps one at a time until it is easy for you to do them all in a matter of seconds. So, if you successfully nail the "Notice" stage, but don't always manage to pull off the "Interrupt" stage, don't give up. Keep noticing until you are able to move to the next step, and know it is all adding up in your favor.

In other words, give yourself grace and remain committed — with enough persistence and dedication, you will succeed. Remember: it's a numbers game.

Before we dive deep into each step, I have prepared a summary of the steps below so you can return to these pages anytime and easily refresh your memory.

## STEP 1: Declare Your Intent

For this Blueprint to work, it is essential that your conscious mind and your subconscious mind are aligned on your goals. Your subconscious mind is referencing the entire archive of your life — your likes, dislikes, patterns, actions, emotions, and associations — so it may not be easily convinced that you wish to make a big change in your life. In this step, I will outline techniques grounded in neuroscience to help you effectively align with your subconscious so you can work together to achieve happiness.

## STEP 2: (Train Yourself to) Notice

It is impossible to switch your negative thought patterns around if you don't know they're occurring in the first place. If you have lived most of your life accepting your thoughts as natural, correct, and unchangeable, awareness of your thoughts is something that can be tricky to get a handle on. In this step, I will outline the things you can look out for to help clue you into when a negative pattern has been engaged. These include physiological cues, word choice, tuning into your emotions, and looking out for assumptions or mind reading.

## STEP 3: Interrupt the Negative Pattern

Because negative thought patterns narrow our focus and often trigger an emotional response, it is difficult to access the rational parts of our brain while negativity has us in its grip. This vital step is designed to create some space between you and your negative thought pattern so that you can access the higher functioning parts of your brain. Techniques include battle breaths, surroundings scan, and body scans. These techniques have one thing in common: they bring you into the present moment. This works because oftentimes negative thought patterns occur when we are perfectly safe, where the only thing that is causing our distress is our own thoughts. Centering ourselves in the present moment will help you perform the final steps.

## STEP 4: Investigate

In this Blueprint, the goal is to live in harmony with your conscious and subconscious mind. Your subconscious mind has a reason for why it is making negative associations and thought patterns, and to successfully rewire these patterns we must take into consideration *why* they are happening in the first place. If we skip this step, we risk the possibility of gaslighting ourselves — creating discontinuity between our conscious and subconscious selves. The positive results, if any, will be fleeting. This step will outline the paths you can take to investigate your negative thought patterns, so that the next step will be as impactful as possible, leading to a strong and lasting neural network that works for you instead of against you.

## STEP 5: Reframe -> Rewire, AKA Tell Yourself a Better Story

This step is where all the magic happens when it comes to training your brain to prefer positivity. This is where you take what you discovered in the Investigate step and use it to tell yourself a better story about whatever it is that triggered your negative thought pattern. There are three essential components of telling yourself a better story. When done successfully, your story must be: (1) positive, (2) actionable, and (3) reality-based. It must be positive because this is how we broaden our perspectives, reality-based because we want to be realistic about the real-world context or constraints that exist, and actionable because this gives us a much-desired sense of control. The reason this works so well is because our brains believe what we tell it — especially if it is a consistent message and backed up with actions that reinforce the message.

## STEP 6: Repeat

Since training your brain to prefer positivity is a numbers game, it is essential that you repeat these steps anytime you catch yourself falling into a negative thought pattern. It will be difficult at first, as you are forging new neural pathways, but remember that your brain likes shortcuts. With enough repetition your brain will catch on and start doing this work for you at a subconscious level.

Now you are primed and ready to jump into the full process! Take your time and be as patient with yourself as you would when teaching a child how to ride a bike. Remember that mastering a bicycle often requires bravery and a willingness to get up and try again after you get thrown off balance.

## (8.1)

# STEP 1: DECLARE YOUR INTENT

*Step one is to use* your conscious mind to communicate your intent to be happy and think more positively to your subconscious mind. You might be thinking this seems unnecessary, or even frivolous. You might be thinking, "Adam, I'm already reading this book. I already know I want to be happy. Isn't that enough?"

Not so fast.

Consciously you may have the desire to be more positive, but statistically speaking you likely have a long-established pattern of negative thinking. This means your subconscious mind is already wired for negativity, and it will not be easily convinced that you want to change. As we will discuss, your subconscious mind does the lion's share of the thinking for you, so it is imperative to align your conscious desire with your subconscious instincts. Reading a book may not be enough to adequately declare your intent.

Your subconscious mind is an abstract entity, and communicating with it effectively sometimes requires some finesse. If you have ever had a dream, you have experienced the peculiar communication style of the subconscious. Techniques successfully utilized in disciplines like Neuro-Linguistic Programming (NLP) provide a good template for the best ways to communicate with our subconscious. NLP stresses the importance of stimulating three main senses as part of our communication process — the visual, auditory, and kinesthetic (feeling) senses — in order to maximize our success in communicating with our own minds.

Think of your subconscious like a supercomputer, with you the user at the keyboard providing inputs representing the conscious mind. This supercomputer has been programmed over the course of your lifetime and is completely unique to the user at the keyboard. It has taken in your experiences, emotions, observed patterns, created associations, and has constructed a mind map with billions of connections that are all available for reference within microseconds. The subconscious is capable of taking in 11 million bits of data per second. Because of its massive computing power, your subconscious is the part of your mind that is responsible for rendering your entire reality: the sights, sounds, smells, and everything else.

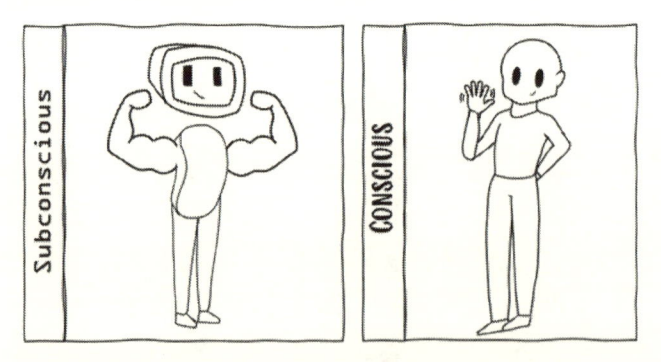

Figure 4 — Subconscious as a Super Computer and the conscious as the User

You on the other hand — the user, the conscious mind — are only capable of processing 40 to 50 bits of data per second. It is the job of your supercomputer subconscious to decide which 40 to 50 bits of data to serve you up at any given time for your conscious consideration. In the absence of any other intentional inputs, it uses the patterns and trends of your entire life to decide what you might want to pay attention to.

If you want a simple way to test this for yourself, stand up (bonus points for doing this right now!) and balance on one foot with your eyes open. As an adult, this should be an easy task long since logged in your motor functions archive. Now, close your eyes and try to maintain your balance. Unless you have put a lot of time and effort into maintaining your balance with your eyes closed, you will struggle to stay on one foot. Consciously you know you want to balance, but you can't with your eyes closed. Why? Because your supercomputer needs the visual inputs to help orient and send signals to the rest of your body.

It is because of the nature and complexity of the subconscious and the important role it plays in our lives that you must clearly and insistently declare your intent to live a more positive and happy life.

Your subconscious is a neutral entity — it wants what you want. You are, in fact, the most interesting and important thing in its existence. It wants to protect you and give you what you want regardless of whether it is good or bad for you. So, when your thoughts are always skewing negative, it is going to "help" you by continuing to draw your attention to all the negative things around you.

Figure 5 – Your subconscious likes whatever you do most

Humans have made it this far by being very aware and tuned into danger, which is why it gives negativity extra emphasis in our minds. This is known as negativity bias. The result is a tendency to let the positive things blend into the backgrounds of our lives, creating a kind of positivity blindness. For the vast majority of people, positive experiences tend to outweigh the negative, however our minds give more emphasis to the negative thoughts. We ruminate on and relive bad things that happen to us, instead of dwelling on the daily positive experiences that are far more frequent.

If negative experiences outnumbered positive ones in reality as much as they do in our thoughts, the world would be unlivable. The fact that a vast majority of the population can live day-to-day peaceful lives, drink clean water, sleep in a bed, and easily acquire food that is safe (and even delicious!) to consume is a testament to the true balance of positive to negative experiences. It doesn't get much more important than safety, food, and shelter.

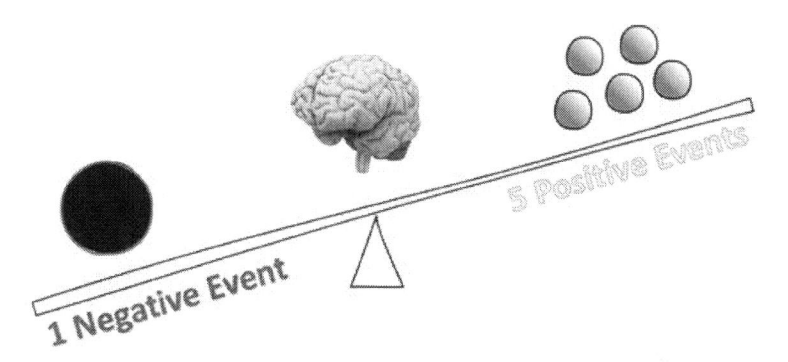

Figure 6 – Negativity Bias / Positivity Blindness

To begin the process of shifting negative thought patterns into positive thought patterns, take a moment to share this goal with your subconscious. Use more than just words; words can be misconstrued by your supercomputer's programming. Try this instead: close your eyes and imagine hovering over your head is a big neon yellow smiley face. Imagine a smile both curving your lips and crinkling your eyes. Picture yourself paying attention to things that bring you joy or serenity, like seeing the excitement of your child experiencing something amazing for the first time, or peacefully watching waves crash onto a white-sand shore. Spend as much time as you need to feel a great swell of positivity.

When you're ready, imagine yourself standing at a fork in the road, one path brightly lit and colorful, and the other dark and ominous. Draw your mind's eye towards the bright path and picture a bright green checkmark hovering in the middle of the path heading in that direction. Look to the dark path and picture a bright red X hovering in the middle of the path going that direction.

For maximum effect, get your other senses into the mix. Imagine a pleasant smell gently emanating from the bright path — the scent of freshly baked bread, or a spring rain shower. Conjure the sounds of Christmas bells or the infectious laughter of children coming from the bright path. Do the opposite for the dark path, imagining the stench of a sewer or red tide. Imagine the screeching of tires or nails on a chalkboard in the distance down the dark path.

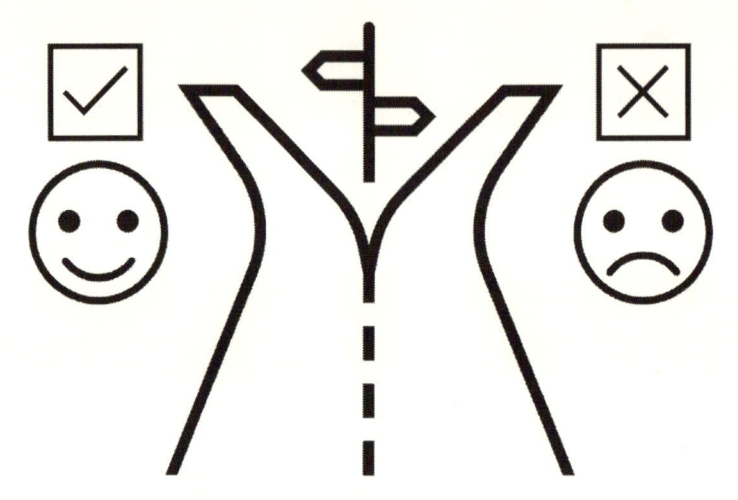

Figure 7 — Visualize choosing the positive path

Now, imagine yourself taking the first few steps towards the bright path, and continue on while leaving the dark path far behind. Once you have walked down the bright path, reset yourself at the fork in the road and repeat the process of walking down the bright path. Do this multiple times until you feel like the message is clear: going forward, I want my attention to be drawn to positive things and aspects of my life.

Using these techniques, you have effectively declared your intent in a way that your subconscious mind will understand. You will need to reinforce this intent with the rest of the process for your mind to build a preference for positivity.

This is a wonderful first step, and you should celebrate your successful execution of it!

**PRACTICAL APPLICATION #5**

After completing this exercise, take five minutes to jot down notes about your experience, what it felt like for you, and what you noticed.

## (8.2)

# STEP 2: (TRAIN YOURSELF TO) NOTICE

*Now that you have* successfully declared your intent, your next task is to train yourself how to notice when a negative thought or emotion is occurring. Most of the groundwork for both negative thoughts and emotions happen at a subconscious level. As a result, most people live their whole lives without questioning the thoughts or emotions they are having. These things simply happen, and because they have been happening a certain way for so long, we tend to think of them as "natural" or "right" or even "uncontrollable."

The truth is your thoughts are one of the few things you have a great deal of control over. When you embrace this truth, it becomes a comforting exercise to be aware and intentional about how you think and respond to the world. Awareness starts with noticing.

## PHYSIOLOGICAL CUES

Luckily, the subconscious has a predictable way of communicating with us, and that is through our bodies in the form of physiological responses. Our involuntary systems like heart rate, breathing, and even perspiration are all within the domain of the subconscious. When it senses a threat or discomfort, it is going to pull on one of the many strings at its disposal to get your attention so that you can take action to stop whatever it is that is bothering you, or to create distance between you and whatever that dangerous or irritable thing is.

Ironically, sometimes the negative thought patterns that trigger these responses are responsible for the negative reaction in the first place.

Here is a quick list of responses that you can tune into as a way to notice when a negative thought or emotion is dominating your mind:

- A desire to lash out
- A desire to retreat
- Blushing / flushing of the face, ears, or chest
- Chest pain or tightness
- Clenched muscles / jaw
- Faster breathing
- Feeling isolated
- Feeling small
- Flared nostrils
- Hyperactivity
- Increased heart rate
- Scowling
- Stomach pain
- Stuttering
- Sudden fatigue
- Sudden hunger
- Sudden lack of appetite
- Sweaty palms
- Talking faster than usual
- Talking louder than usual

Your responses to negative thoughts or feelings will be unique to you, and because our negative thought patterns tend to be on repeat, you should be able to spot a pattern once you start paying attention.

Noticing in the moment can be difficult, and it may not be until later when you're looking back on your day that you spot a time when negativity had you in its grip and you failed to notice. That's okay — noticing in retrospect is just as useful as noticing in the moment. This way, you can alert your subconscious that the next time a certain feeling occurs, you want to notice.

To create this alignment with your subconscious, use a similar visualization technique that we used in the previous step. Close your eyes and imagine yourself in the moment of negativity. Focus your attention on whatever physiological response you were having, your heart thumping hard, for example. Imagine hearing the thuds and feeling the pounding against your rib cage. Now picture yourself placing a hand over your heart and taking a deep breath as the thudding slows to a gentle and steady rhythm.

Not only does this visualization technique inform your subconscious of your desire to notice this particular response, it is also a form of rehearsal, giving your subconscious an idea of how you wish to respond the next time it happens. Rehearsal and visual, auditory, and kinesthetic (VAK) techniques are commonly used in a discipline known as Neuro-Linguistic Programming (NLP). NLP has developed over many years to help practitioners better collaborate with their minds and improve their lives. Curious readers can find a recommended text to learn more about NLP in the References section of this book.

## WORD CHOICE

Another way that you can train yourself to notice negative thoughts is to pay particular attention to your word choice. Words can have nuance depending on who is using them; however, there are some universal truths that can be counted on when it comes to the kinds of words people use every day. The words to look out for are self-limiting words that put boundaries around what you can do, think, or feel.

Words like "can't," "shouldn't," or "should" imply some kind of gate keeping. So, when you hear these words come up in your thinking, make it a habit to ask yourself, "Why can't I? Who is stopping me?" "Shouldn't? Says who?" Whose voice are you actually hearing? A parent, past teacher, or your own?

Words like, "have to" or "must" imply some outside force is making you think, feel, or do things in a certain way. Again, the remedy to this type of thinking is to question who set those parameters, if they are reasonable or even accurate, and if they should apply to you at all.

Absolutist language like "always," "never," "all," or "nothing" are equally important to look out for. This type of language means you are generalizing, and in a world with so much nuance and wiggle room, the odds are that whatever it is you are thinking about is not as black or white as you are trying to make it. Question absolutist language with a healthy dose of skepticism: is it *really* true that *all* pit bulls are aggressive? Absolutist language can even limit you if you use it positively; saying that you're always going to be on time, for example, creates some undue cognitive dissonance when some unexpected delay causes you to be late to an important event. Absolutist language doesn't leave the wiggle room required to give yourself grace and is indicative of rigid thinking that cannot adapt with the constant changes that life tends to bring us.

Finally, be on the lookout for words that generally have negative connotations. Words like bad, wrong, stupid, ugly, terrible, mean, bossy, rude, fault, moron. These words imply judgement — a judgement you are making that may or may not be grounded in truth or reality. When you find yourself making these judgements, take a pause and become curious as to why that might be. Oftentimes when we do this, we are projecting our own insecurities or perceived limitations onto others or situations.

## ASSUMPTIONS AND MIND READING

Making assumptions is something our brains love to do — it is a predictive organ and by its very nature goes out of its way to guess what will happen at any given time to ensure you are safe and prepared for whatever comes your way. Assumptions imply that you are operating off limited information, and yet many people use their assumptions to live their lives and inform their thoughts, beliefs, and behaviors. Because of our inherent negativity bias, assumptions often reinforce our negative beliefs, contributing to the imbalance between positive and negative thoughts. Learning how to spot when you are making an assumption goes a long way towards satisfying the Notice step of this process. Words to keep an eye out for here are "probably," "bet," and "guess."

Similar to assumptions, it can be helpful to pay attention to when you try to fill in the blank of what others are thinking. More often than not, attempts to "mind read" in this way are actually projections of our own thoughts. Thoughts like, "S/he doesn't like me, it must be because I'm so awkward," are probably more a reflection of the awkwardness you feel or because of your fear of being awkward or excluded. Not only are you making an assumption about whether or not someone likes you, you take the extra step to presume that you know the reason for why that might be.

> "I've lived through some terrible things in my life. Some of them actually happened."
> — Mark Twain

## TUNE INTO YOUR EMOTIONS

Emotions are another way that your subconscious communicates with you. Emotions are a powerful tool that your brain uses to encode memories, make associations, and inform your decisions. The challenge can be that many emotional associations were created when you were a child with limited rationalization abilities. Unless you have made the conscious effort to update your emotional associations, there's a good chance your emotional patterns are startling similar to those you had when you were a seven-year-old child.

To help you take better notice of your negative emotions, take a look at the basic emotions wheel in Figure 8 on the next page. More complex wheels can be found through a simple google search. An emotions wheel begins at the center with basic emotions: sadness, fear, anger, disgust, happiness, and surprise. From there, subcategories radiate out. For example, subcategories for anger can include let down, humiliated, bitter, mad, aggressive, frustrated, distant, and critical. There is a third band that further expounds on these subcategories, but you get the idea. We experience a range of emotions, but they typically all come back to the basic six emotions already mentioned. As part of this step, the emotions you'll want to be on the lookout for are sad, bad, fearful, angry, and disgusted.

When you notice any of these emotions have been triggered, it is time to move onto the next step: Interrupt the Negative Pattern.

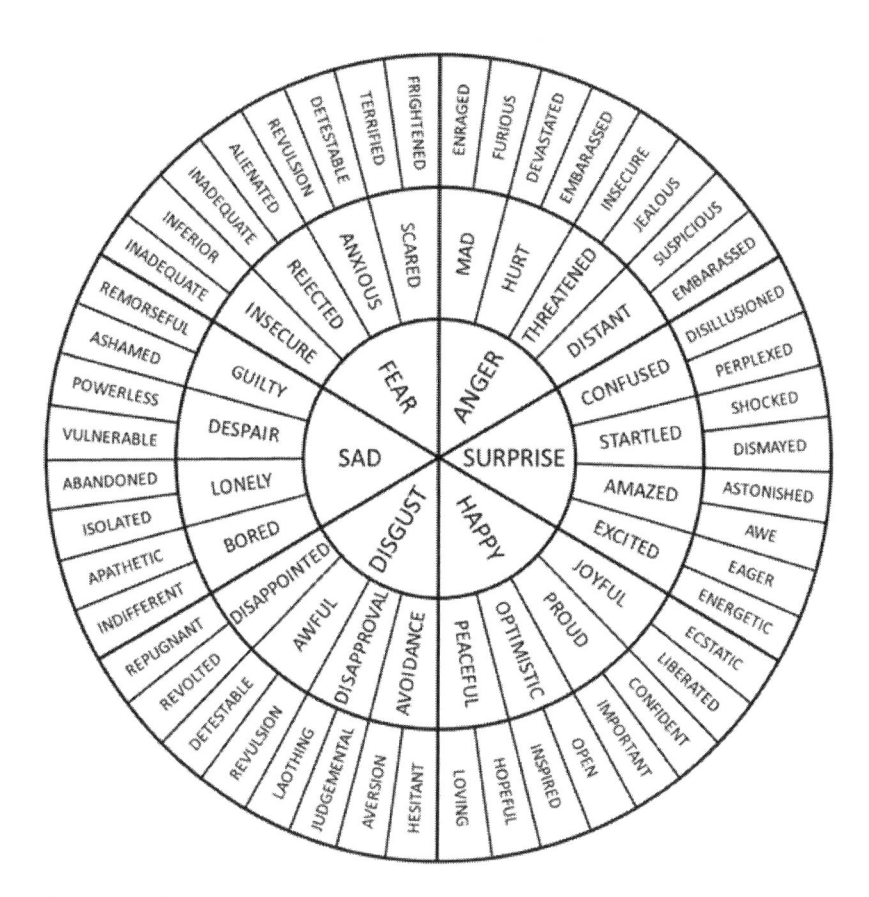

Figure 8 — Emotions Wheel

## THE INNER CRITIC

One of the first things I noticed once I became more aware of my self-talk was how mean I was. I would chastise myself for things I didn't do right or blame myself for misfortunes that, in reality, I could have done nothing about. I remember being startled by how harsh I was and began to adopt a process that helped calm these thoughts down. When I caught my inner critic speaking, I would counter with a friendly thought along the lines of, "Hey bro. It's okay. Take it easy." This helped immensely and resulted in an overall calming of my nerves until one day the critic retired completely.

The reason we have an inner critic is well-intentioned enough: the inner critic wants us to be happy but has a warped view of how to make that happen. It believes happiness is achieved through things like perfection or not trying anything hard as to avoid failure completely. It has become harsh through some maladaptive coping mechanism likely developed when we were young. Critics may even take the form of someone in your life who was especially harsh to you, and you hear their words when you feel like you're not measuring up or want to try something new or risky.

Training yourself to notice when your inner critic is driving your negative thought patterns will allow you to open a dialog with that inner critic, and to eventually make a friend of the critic. Look out for times where you are blaming and shaming yourself, putting yourself down, or telling yourself you can't succeed. These are all signs that your inner critic is at the helm and needs to be talked into a more reasonable position.

## PRACTICAL APPLICATION #6

Take a few minutes to jot down notes on what some of your common physiological responses are, what words to watch for, and what emotions are most associated with your typical negative thoughts.

**Physiological responses**

**Negative, limiting, or judgmental words to watch for**

**Emotions to pay attention to**

## (8.3)

# STEP 3: INTERRUPT THE NEGATIVE PATTERN

*Once you have noticed* your negative thought or emotion, you must now interrupt the pattern so that you can prepare yourself to walk down that bright path instead of the dark one. As Professor Fredrickson has proven, negative thoughts and emotions narrow our mindsets, and make it extremely difficult to see alternatives in a situation that is causing the negative reaction. As a result, it is necessary to interrupt this narrowing before moving forward.

Luckily for me and you, this is a very simple thing to do. As simple as breathing — in this case, literally. My personal preferred method of interrupting negativity is to engage in a series of battle breaths.

## BATTLE BREATHS

"Battle breaths" have been coined as such due to their use by the Navy SEALs. The SEALs use battle breaths to help graduate initiates from their program, and I imagine later to keep nerves in check during extremely strenuous situations. Before battle breaths were introduced to the SEALs program, the Navy had a hard time graduating anyone into this elite unit. Since the instructors were certain they were not asking initiates to do anything that was physically impossible, they invited Navy doctors to observe and make recommendations on how to build the necessary resilience to pass the program.

The solution? Battle breaths.

A battle breath consists of a six second inhale, two second hold, and a six second exhale. Repeat. The long out breath slows the heart rate, while the long in breath fills the lungs and floods the muscles and brain with oxygen. The net result in a physiological reset, allowing whatever panic or distress that had narrowed the focus of the initiate to be interrupted and the rational, conscious part of the brain to pick up where it left off.

The results? Navy SEAL graduates capable of withstanding the most grueling of situations.

So, if it can work for the Navy SEALs, it can definitely work for you. It certainly has for me. In fact, I found that after enough regular use I had become so adept at noticing my body's cues — a tense jaw and shoulders — that I would hear the first deep in-breath before I realized that I'd needed one. I had trained myself so well to notice my discomfort and respond to it in a predictable way that my subconscious was both the initiator of the physical response to my negative thoughts and the interpreter of those same thoughts.

In other words, I hit the tipping point to where my mind recognized the new pattern I'd created and fired it by default instead of consulting my conscious mind. This is precisely what I mean when I say that it takes work to make these changes, but gets much easier over time.

## SURROUNDINGS SCAN

Another method to interrupt your negative thought patterns is to perform a surroundings scan. This one is just as simple as breathing, requiring nothing more than taking a few seconds to look around at your immediate surroundings. Notice the paint color if you're indoors, or the types of foliage on a nearby tree if you are outdoors. Take in the lighting and how it casts shadows; focus on small details of objects around you.

This method works because despite the claims on many a résumé, human beings are not actually that good at multitasking. It also works because the brain's favorite place to be is in the present moment: it doesn't have to try to integrate your anxiety and worry with whatever is happening externally to make up a complete memory. By focusing on the here and now, you are interrupting the negative thought patterns that were taking your mind further and further away from the present moment.

## BODY SCAN

Different from a surroundings scan, a body scan requires you to direct your focus inward. As mentioned before, your subconscious oversees all your involuntary systems, and as a result it is always monitoring the status of your body. You are always aware of the big toe on your right foot, for example, it is just most of the time you are only subconsciously aware. By turning your conscious focus onto the different parts of your body — toes, feet, heels, ankles, calves, etc. — you are interrupting the negative thought patterns that have dominated your thought process.

A body scan may also supplement the step of noticing: for example you might notice a pounding heart associated with your negative thoughts, but upon engaging in a body scan you also notice that your hands are clenched at the same time. Use this opportunity to relax what is tight and feel fully embodied, focusing on the feeling of your weight in a chair if you are sitting, or the feeling of the ground beneath your feet if you are standing. Wiggle your toes and focus on the sensation. Roll your shoulders and envision every intricate connection of your muscles.

## COMPASSIONATE SELF TALK & GRATITUDE

Compassion has a way of stopping negativity in its tracks, and this can be just as true for your interior world as it is for the exterior world. When you notice a negative thought pattern start up, interrupt it with words of kindness and grace for yourself or the situation. Acknowledge the feelings, tell yourself it is okay to have them, and that you're doing your best and you're going to get through whatever the situation is. You may even adopt a term of affection for yourself like "buddy," "friend," or "brother/sister." Using this kind of self-talk is a way of communicating to your triggered supercomputer brain that there is a place of safety. That place of safety is within you, and you can access it at any time with compassionate self-talk.

You may also consider leveraging thoughts of gratitude to help interrupt a negative thought pattern. If you find yourself feeling down on your luck, you can pause and take a moment to silently express gratitude that the situation isn't worse, or that you have a friend or family member to lean on. You can even be grateful for something that has nothing to do with your current situation — like having clean water to drink or a warm place to sleep — and you will be equally as successful in interrupting your negative thought pattern. For gratitude to be as effective as possible in interrupting negative patterns, try to be creative and come up with new things you are grateful for each time you use this interruption technique.

## FIRE AN ANCHOR

An anchor is another NLP technique designed to trigger a pleasant memory or feeling at-will. You can build an anchor by focusing your mind on a pleasant memory or feeling and tying that memory to a physical gesture or touch. For example, if I wanted to encode a feeling of achievement into a trigger, I would think of a time where I was recognized for my good work at an award ceremony. I would transport myself back to that time and place in my mind's eye and recall the pleasant feelings of being called on stage to receive my award. At the peak of that pleasant memory, I could run the index finger of my right hand from the base to the tip of my pinky finger on my left hand.

This quick gesture is not something I would do as a part of my normal mannerisms, but is also not so out of the ordinary that it would be observed as strange behavior to others who might see me do it. To encode this anchor, I must conjure the memory and feelings associated with it multiple times — each time at the peak of the good feeling — repeating the gesture until I can perform the gesture and feel the feeling without the effort of conjuring it.

Once you have an anchor or two encoded, firing them is as simple as performing the gesture. Firing the same anchor is not something you want to do often, as the effects will fade with overuse.

This method can be especially helpful in interrupting particularly strong negative thoughts or emotions. It is also a useful technique because it primes the brain for positivity, which is the foundation for setting the conditions for happiness.

---

FUN FACT! BY TRYING EACH OF THESE EXERCISES ONCE YOU ARE CREATING THE VERY FIRST NEURON CONNECTOR. AS YOU REPEAT THESE TECHNIQUES, THE CONNECTIONS WILL STRENGTHEN. BONUS FUN FACT: READING UPSIDE DOWN HELPS BUILD NEUROPLASTICITY!

**PRACTICAL APPLICATION #7**

Practice each one of the Interruption techniques, and then take a few moments to jot down notes about which one feels the best to you. Describe how it felt when practicing the techniques. Refer back to your list of physiological cues, word choices, and emotions on page 63, to look out for and map which interruption response you might want to use when you notice each common response.

**Battle Breaths**




**Surroundings Scan**




**Body Scan**




**Compassionate Self Talk & Gratitude**

## (8.4)

# STEP 4: INVESTIGATE

*Once you have noticed* your negative thoughts or emotions, and you have successfully interrupted the pattern, the next step is to investigate what has triggered the thoughts or emotions in the first place.

Knowing the *why* will help make the next step as powerful and effective as possible. Not only will we be looking for the trigger and root cause in this step, but we will also take the time to examine your perception versus reality, as well as ask the all-important question: "Do I have control over this situation?"

This step of the process will likely take the longest to master, and in the beginning is probably one you will have to do in retrospect rather than in the moment. Understanding yourself to this level requires the courage to look inward and honestly assess the programming that has been formed across your entire lifetime. Leverage the Notice step to earmark situations you need to investigate when you have more time, a quiet place, and the mental resources to genuinely explore your inner workings. In my experience, the best breakthroughs come hours after the event in the form of shower thoughts. You know the kind: the perfect response or insight that forms hours removed from the event or situation while you are doing something completely unrelated. So be open and receptive in those regular periods of mental rest.

It may also be the case that, due to natural blind spots, you need help to fully investigate your reactions and responses to certain situations. Consider reaching out to a trusted friend or relative who can help you talk through your experiences. Alternatively, traditional talk therapy can be very helpful in uncovering the origin stories for your day-to-day feelings and behaviors. The key is to gain as much insight and perspective as possible so that you use the knowledge to inform the next step of this process: telling yourself a better story.

## THE TRIGGER

Using the Investigation step to understand more about what has triggered you will set you up for success in the overall process. Knowing what triggers you allows you to avoid future negative situations altogether, and when you can't avoid them, it helps you be able to respond faster in the moment until eventually the trigger has no impact on you whatsoever.

Sometimes triggers can be a person or a place that your brain has flagged as anywhere from troublesome to traumatizing. Their mere presence may set your thought patterns down the dark path, so the more you understand and can acknowledge the trigger, the more adept you will be at addressing the concerns that your subconscious mind has.

Triggers can also form as a result of certain topics, confrontation in general, or when the right confluence of factors occur to impact your mood in a negative way. Perhaps not having plans on a Friday night makes you feel isolated and starts you down a path of negativity. Maybe you get along with someone just fine, right up until they bring up *that* topic. It could be that anytime someone makes an observation about your work you find yourself reacting negatively.

Once you have a good sense of what triggers you, the next step is to investigate the root cause, which can be far removed from the actual trigger.

## ROOT CAUSE

Most of the time, negative thoughts and feelings can be attributed to a single root cause: not feeling safe. Safety is the topmost concern of your brain. We live in a world in which anything can happen, and the not-so-vigilant can find their stay here on earth cut abruptly short. This has been historically accurate for the millennia-plus of human existence, and while still true, premature death or severe injury is not lurking around every corner the way it used to be. The reason we can still treat everyday challenges like a life-and-death situation is because evolution takes a long time, and our brains are still adjusting to the rapidly changing environments in which we find ourselves.

On top of that evolutionary holdover, many of the feelings, associations, and understandings of the world we have today were developed when we were children between the ages of zero and seven years old, before our brains were even fully developed, and in some cases before we had language centers in our brains to comprehend or to give words to what was happening to us. Many of us are operating on programming that was written when we were young, and only limitedly updated as needed and as we are exposed to new things and perspectives as adults.

For this reason, the root cause of why you feel a certain way may be something you need to search for in your childhood or early adulthood. Does the scent of Old Spice trigger you because it is what your verbally abusive grandfather wore? Is your sense of helplessness the result of being repressed as a child in a strict household, and so you have trouble finding your voice as an adult? Perhaps in place of speaking up, you tell yourself a negative story about what would happen if you did and in doing so rob yourself of finding out if your past experiences accurately predict outcomes in your adult life. These childhood associations are likely to be alive and well in your subconscious mind as if they could have occurred yesterday. Your subconscious mind has taken specific note of them because they are associated with strong negative emotions, which are associated with danger.

The way feelings of insecurity manifest can be complex and unique to each individual. For example, someone may get disproportionately defensive over criticism of their work because they perceive that it puts their employment status in jeopardy. That leads to the next thought, and then the next: if they become unemployed, they won't be able to pay their bills, and if they can't pay their bills, they may become homeless. Another person may feel negative about their physical appearance because they fear it will mean they will never find a partner, which means they do not belong to a group and not belonging to a group has been encoded in our DNA to spark feelings of danger and threat.

This negative thought spiral takes a person from a relatively inconsequential occurrence — criticism of your work for example — to a place of fight-or-flight with surprising speed. And, as we know, negativity narrows our ability to think and explore alternative solutions to our problems. This is why the Interrupt step is so key in our ability to shift these patterns.

When you are in the root-cause phase of the investigation step, start by asking yourself what you are feeling unsafe about. Examine in which ways that feeling is manifesting and ask yourself if your response seems to be proportional to whatever it is that has triggered this feeling or thought. The odds are that the threat is not as great as your initial thought pattern has made it out to be.

## EXAMINE THE FACTS

Once you have a handle on what has triggered your negative thoughts or emotions and its root cause, go on to ask yourself if your fears are well founded, or if you are tumbling down the slippery slope of a negative thought spiral. Will you really be fired over a single criticism of your work? What resources or factors are working in your favor? Are you ignoring the positive aspects of the situation and giving bias towards the negative ones? Is there a trend forming a pattern? If so, can you address them before the trend plays itself to its ultimate conclusion?

Because you interrupted the negative thought pattern, examining the facts should be easier to do from a more objective standpoint. To help in keeping this step as neutral as possible, try to zoom out from the situation; look at yourself from the perspective of a third party. How would someone who didn't know anything about the situation — or your fears and triggers — perceive the situation? How would they assess the facts?

If your negative thought patterns have been triggered by a specific person, switch yourself from the perspective of an objective bystander to that specific person to see if you can imagine the situation from their perspective. What do they see and what might they be feeling in that moment? This will help you assess the facts from multiple angles, giving you more information to address your negative thought patterns even more effectively.

## WHAT IS MY NEGATIVE RESPONSE DOING FOR ME?

Another aspect of the investigation step is to ask yourself: what is my negative response doing for me? What am I gaining from complaining about something I don't like? What does it get me to become angry over something I see on the news?

I believe the answer to this question is firmly grounded in good intentions. Becoming angry over injustice is a way to feel like you care, and that you are a good person — because you are! But you don't need to be angry or outraged for that to be true. People often become upset when they feel slighted because it puts into question the quality of their character.

> **"Holding onto anger is like drinking poison and expecting the other person to die."**
> — Buddha

Oftentimes, the way people treat you or behave is more of a reflection of who they are, where they are at in their lives, and their own insecurities rather than a reflection on you. This can be easy to overlook because we are naturally self-centered, and I don't mean that in a negative context. The only perspective we truly know is our own. When we fill in the inevitable gaps, our preference for positive or negative thinking has a significant impact on how we experience life.

If you think your negative response is doing anything positive for you, I urge you to think twice. More often than not, all it gets you is higher blood pressure and isolation. In these instances, remind yourself that you can still be a good person without getting angry or bitter. Becoming angry or bitter is what diminishes your ability to live a happy life, and what good is that doing in the grand scheme of things?

## CONTROL

Now that you know the trigger, root cause, and have examined both the facts and what your reaction is doing for you, ask yourself if whatever has triggered your negative thoughts or feelings is something you have control over.

This is an easy question to answer because what you have control over is extremely, *extremely* finite. As a reformed control freak, this was a realization that shifted my entire world view — for the better. What you have control over is yourself. Your thoughts, behaviors, and words you use to speak to others and yourself. What you do not have control over is literally everything else.

Bifurcating the question of control in this way was life changing for me, and simplified things in a way that gave me a lot of my own mental resources back. Before I passed everything that was bothering me through this filter of "can I control this or can I not?" I spent a lot of my time being angry about things I had no control over, from other people's decisions and life choices to the policy decisions and tomfoolery playing out at a national level. I used to think, "This person is making me mad!" After I internalized the knowledge that I can only control myself, I came to realize that not only had I been giving up my power over the one thing I could actually control, but it was *me* that was allowing *me* to be mad. No one can make me feel a certain way — that is in my hands, and my hands alone.

Figure 9 – Scope of Control Flow

Another benefit to looking at situations through the control lens is that if the answer to the question of if you can control a situation comes back as "No," it fundamentally changes the way in which you will move forward. When you incorrectly assess that you can control a situation and your inevitable failure comes, you are more likely to become angry and confrontational. If, instead, you acknowledge that you cannot control the situation but still wish to have a different outcome, you can approach the situation from a place of *influence* instead of control. Influence is a cooperative mindset, one that requires the wielder of influence to take into consideration what other people might want or need in addition to your own end goal. Influence requires you to consider the situation from multiple perspectives and opens your mind to new potential pathways. Thinking in terms of influence broadens your perspective, a central aspect of positive thinking. Adding this question of control to the Investigate step simplifies the way forward and paves the way to flourishing.

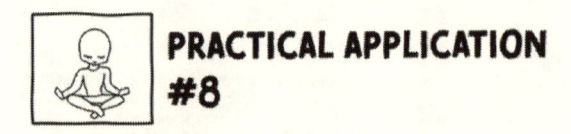

## PRACTICAL APPLICATION #8

## PUTTING IT ALL TOGETHER

An investigation is a series of questions that lead you to a conclusion. When in doubt, the following questions can be used as a jumping off point for this step. To help you with the concept, I have provided answers from a personal example of not feeling heard at work. Pick your own example and fill in the answers to the questions next to my answers to get used to using this method.

| | | | |
|---|---|---|---|
| 1 | Q: | What did I notice? | |
| | A: | The whininess in my voice when I reacted in the moment. | |

| 2 | Q: | What was the trigger and what was the result? |
|---|---|---|
|   | A: | When my suggestions were not considered at work, I felt angry and annoyed. |
| 3 | Q: | Why did it bother me so much? (Root cause) |
|   | A: | It made me feel like a helpless kid again to not be listened to. |
| 4 | Q: | What was my response doing for me? |
|   | A: | I thought that I could get what I want if I tried hard enough. I wanted control. |
| 5 | Q: | Can I control other people? |
|   | A: | No. |
| 6 | Q: | Can I influence other people? |
|   | A: | Yes, and whining is probably the least effective influencing tool! |

As we have discussed, many negative thought patterns are different versions of the same thought repeated, so by answering the questions to one negative pattern you may find yourself able to transfer the insights you uncover to other negative patterns you encounter. The work you do in this step will go a long way to boosting your self-awareness and ability to make different choices using your rational rather than emotional mind.

**PRACTICAL APPLICATION #9**

Create a list or jot down some key words for each of the following. Use what you've written to help you map a root cause to your known triggers. Are you undermining your own intentions, for example? Are you trying to control the uncontrollable? Is your childhood experience informing your adult contemporary life?

Your known triggers

What intentions do you operate with normally?

What are your controllables in your life?

What are the uncontrollables in your life?

What are some things that bothered or troubled you as a child?

## (8.5)

# STEP 5: REFRAME -> REWIRE, AKA TELL YOURSELF A BETTER STORY

***This is where the real magic*** of the Blueprint to Happy occurs. In order to gain the benefits of positive thought patterns, we must ensure they become the default operating mode of our minds. The way we do that is by outnumbering our negative thoughts with positive ones until our brains can catch on and perform the process for us automatically.

Now that you have trained yourself to notice when a negative thought pattern has been triggered, interrupted the pattern, and investigated the origin of the negative thoughts, you can use this information to tell yourself a better story. That is what it means to reframe — to look at something from a different perspective. Because the brain believes what we tell it to believe, it will have no reason to question this new frame, especially if it is in line with your actions and behavior. When you consistently reframe previously negative outlooks, you are actively rewiring your brain to prefer positivity.

The most effective way to reframe, or to tell yourself a better story, is to ensure it includes three essential components: it must be positive, actionable, and reality-based. I call this the trifecta of how to tell yourself a better story. Let's break down each one of these components to understand them better.

## POSITIVE

This one is a given, considering that we achieve happiness through developing a preference for positivity. By creating reframes that are consistently positive, we are signaling to our subconscious how we would like to view the world, and what we would prefer to have our attention drawn to.

## ACTIONABLE

A successful reframe should be actionable in some way. This satisfies our innate desire to have control in our lives. While we can control very little in the grand scheme of life, we can lean into the power we do have: power over our own thoughts, beliefs, behaviors, and actions. "Actionable" in this context can simply be a choice to smile rather than cry. One of my guiding mantras in life is "If the outcome will remain the same no matter what I do, I'd rather smile than cry." As a result, when I drop something or make a mess, my first reaction is to give a little chuckle before cheerfully cleaning up. This is in stark contrast to the person I was before adopting this mantra — that person was more likely to curse and make the situation worse with a hasty and irritable cleanup. With the help of the Blueprint to Happy, I can realize that the damage has already been done, so why spend precious extra heartbeats being upset in the aftermath?

## REALITY-BASED

Finally, in order to successfully rewire our brains, we have to ensure alignment between our thoughts and the real-world context we are in. Denying reality in favor of positivity is what many probably mean when they refer to "toxic positivity," but I prefer the term "gaslighting" to describe this. Gaslighting is when someone knows the truth, but purposefully constructs a different story and tries to persuade others of this false narrative. That is not the intent of this process, so when you are reframing it's essential that the story you arrive at is reality-based. This way, we're creating further alignment with our inner and outer worlds, increasing our ability to rewire our brains without confusion or reservations that would make it easy to backslide or lose momentum in our efforts.

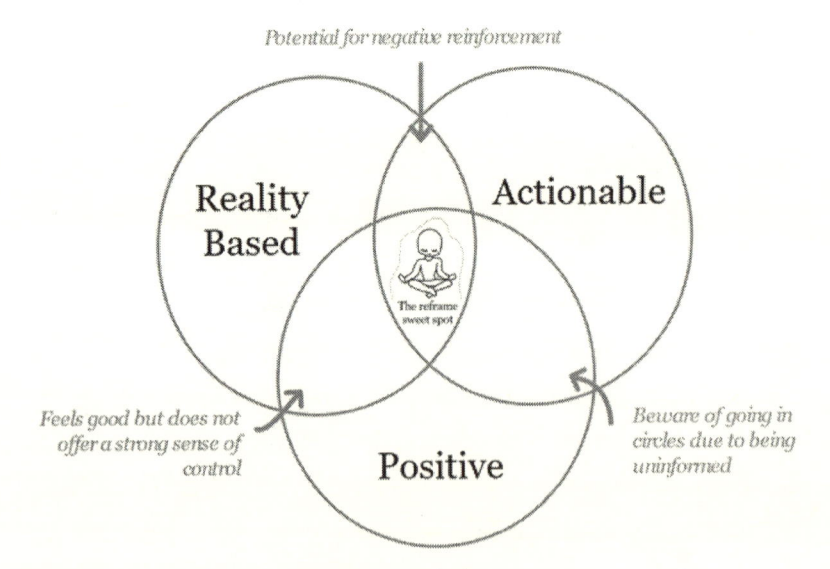

Figure 10 – The trifecta of telling yourself a better story

All three of these components must be present for an effective reframe. If your reframes are positive and reality-based, you may feel better but still lack the sense of control that comes with including an actionable element to your reframe. If you create a reframe that is actionable and reality-based but lacking positivity, you're risking utilizing negative reinforcement to achieve your goals, which has a diminishing rate of return. Finally, if your reframes are positive and actionable but are not reality-based, you risk going in circles or demoralizing yourself when your perspectives do not match up with your surroundings.

Let's look at some real-world examples that may lead to a negative outlook or thought pattern and reframe them using the Trifecta of Telling Yourself a Better Story.

## REFRAMING EXAMPLES

**Situation**: You're running late for an engagement downtown and park in a hurry without paying. When you return to your car, you find that you've received a ticket. It's expensive and you really can't afford the unexpected expense.

**Default Response**: Get angry, curse the parking attendants, begin fretting about how you'll pay when you have a lot of other bills already. Go home and get in a fight with a family member because of your bad mood.

**Reframe**: When you realize you forgot to pay for parking, the ticket makes sense (reality-based). The parking attendant didn't know you were running late and was just doing their job, and luckily your car did not get towed (positive). Next time, you'll be sure to leave earlier, and since it is your first ticket, you can appeal and ask for a warning instead. When you go home, you can ask for a much-needed hug from your family member (actionable).

Using this reframe, you can acknowledge the stress of having to pay for something you weren't expecting, and that your emotional response is because the setback on some level threatens your safety and security. But you also know the ticket doesn't have to be paid for immediately and you may have options like arranging forgiveness or a payment plan through the court. It is inconvenient, but you have learned from the experience and know you'll do better next time. Additionally, instead of damaging your relationship with a family member by letting negativity take over, you can deepen it by embracing positivity instead and seeking comfort instead of confrontation.

**Situation**: You are a member of a marginalized group that is being used as the current political football. When you watch the news, or scroll social media, upsetting messages and narratives seem to be everywhere with no hope in sight for it getting better.

**Default Response**: You feel isolated and angry that we live in such an intolerant society. You feel pity for yourself because you didn't choose to be who you are, and you feel unsafe because of how angry everyone seems to be. You continue consuming the news and engaging on social media because you're not sure what else you can do. You believe it is your duty to be informed and outraged because otherwise it means you don't care.

**Reframe**: Despite the rhetoric, you examine your day-to-day life and realize you have a support network that respects and enjoys time with you (reality-based). You understand that the hate people have in their hearts is a reflection of them, and not you. More than that, you can't really control what people do or think anyway. Being who you are makes you happy and secure (positive). Since the best response to hate and bigotry is to live a happy life, you'll continue being who you are and cut back on the news and social media, focusing more on the things and people in your life that make you happy while also advocating for your best interests as the need arises (actionable).

Using this reframe, you can still make a commitment to advocate for yourself while not getting sucked in or worked up about a whole host of things you cannot control. Acknowledging you cannot control the shifting tides of society's sentiments, legislation, or discrimination does not mean that you accept it. Allowing these things to take you into a negative headspace is one of the most counterproductive things you can do if you wish to see change in the world. Only from a place of positivity will your perspective be broadened enough to see the levers that will be truly impactful for change. Keeping a positive mindset will also make you more likely to reach out and connect with others rather than isolating yourself, and just like changing thought patterns, changing the currents of society is a numbers game. Safety in numbers — not isolation.

**Situation**: You suffer an injury or major health setback and must spend a long time recovering. You may miss work, and you are limited in what you're able to do.

**Default Response**: You feel depressed and isolated because of your situation, fearing that you're missing out on your life. You feel anxiety about having to miss work, and what it will mean for your future. Each day you spend in despair and pain, unhappy and pessimistic.

**Reframe**: You understand the most important thing for you after your setback is to heal so you can get back to living your life fully. While loss of income may be a challenge, you can only do so much while you are recovering — best not to worry about what you can't change. Plus, the people in your life understand and empathize with your situation and may be able to help you get through it (reality-based). You embrace the need to rest, and even appreciate that you'll get an opportunity to slow down for a while, maybe catch up on some books you've been meaning to read or long-forgotten video games (actionable). Not to mention, you're grateful that you are in a place of recovery and that your situation is not long-term. This experience gives you a perspective that helps you enjoy and appreciate life even more once you are fully recovered (positive).

Using this reframe, you've created a much better mental space for healing. Remember when we discussed the benefits of a preference for positivity: putting the mind at ease makes it more willing and able to expend energy healing your body rather than staying in crisis mitigation mode. Worrying about lost income will result in more lost income as it will delay your overall healing process. Additionally, when you view a situation positively, your ability to effectively problem solve is increased and solutions may present themselves along the way as you recover. Giving yourself rest-friendly things to do like read or play video games offers you a sense of control and presents something new for the brain to occupy itself with instead of whatever pain or discomfort you may be in. Finally, by recognizing the positive aspects of your situation, such as your condition not being permanent and the fresh perspective, you are reinforcing your preference for positivity which will make it easier to access on your recovery journey.

**Situation**: Your marriage of many years has ended, leaving you in a position of having to start over. You're intimidated by having to do everything on your own, have limited resources, and don't feel like you have a direction in life.

**Default Response**: You hyper-focus on all the things that scare and worry you, feeling isolated and abandoned. You feel unsatisfied with the downgrade in quality of life you perceive because of your limited resources. You complain often to whoever will listen and spend most of your time trying to numb the pain and discomfort you feel via entertainment, social media, drugs, or alcohol.

**Reframe**: There is a reason your marriage has ended, and ultimately you know it was probably the best thing for the both of you. People grow and sometimes they grow apart. Perhaps there are even some things you need to work on that you couldn't while in that relationship (reality-based). You sit down and take an inventory of all the things you wanted to do, see, or experience that just never happened in your relationship. Keeping these things in mind, you can brainstorm on how and when you can make it all happen, even if it isn't right away (actionable). You tell yourself this is a wonderful opportunity to rediscover who you are, what you want in life, and you feel grateful that you are in a position where you are now able to do so. Whatever was holding you back in the past is gone, and you are free to take your destiny into your own hands without the baggage you had been hauling around (positive).

Using this reframe, you spend no time at all fretting and more time problem solving. You recognize that fretting will just isolate and drag you down. Instead of a setback or a hardship, you view this as an opportunity to fulfill your own needs. This is the road that will lead to healthy and happy companionship if that is what will serve you best, but that road can only be traveled once you understand your own wants and needs. If your attachment to your lost resources were holding you back from trying new things and looking for happiness where you are most likely to find it — inside of you — then this reframe prevents you from wasting your time looking elsewhere. The road to happiness is not paved evenly; it often begins as a bumpy ride but smooths out the more you get the hang of it.

**Situation**: Your management wants to give you more responsibilities that you are not entirely comfortable with. The new scope is not related to anything you've done before, and you don't want to screw it up or get overwhelmed. More than anything, you just want to keep doing what you've been doing already.

**Default Response**: You feel resentful at this uninvited intrusion and want to reject the new work immediately. You express skepticism and displeasure to your leaders and coworkers.

**Reframe**: You acknowledge that what is being asked of you is a stretch, but also that your management felt like you are capable of doing what is asked (reality-based). You are clear with your leaders and coworkers that you are learning and might make mistakes but are open to try new things and grow your abilities. You commit to yourself that you will reach out when help is required (actionable). Learning new things is a great way to obtain additional job security, grow your mental capacity, and increase your skills for future roles (positive).

Using this reframe, you are keeping an open mind about your growing responsibilities and meeting the moment with a smile rather than a frown. This increases your capacity to learn and problem solve, which will be essential in growing your skills. Furthermore, you are not limiting your career progression arbitrarily, as refusing growth now may mean opportunities will not be offered to you in the future. What is being asked of you might be too much — but you will not know that for sure until you begin the work. It is a much easier conversation with leadership to be able to outline why the additional responsibilities are not doable because you have tried and have all the details, versus making assumptions and being able to provide no insight into why the added responsibilities cannot be done. Taking a negative approach will make you appear uncooperative and unhelpful, whereas a positive approach will make you appear confident and capable, even if the outcome *ultimately* remains the same.

## PRACTICAL APPLICATION #10

Are you ready to give it a try? Start by reframing the examples provided below.

**Situation**: You are traveling for a vacation, and due to conditions you cannot control, you are delayed by many hours.

*Hint: You may fill in the blanks based on what is more common for you: would you be traveling with your family, or alone, for example? Are you more likely to travel via plane, personal vehicle, or train?*

**Your reframe**:




**Situation**: Someone you were relying on has failed to deliver on a commitment for you.

*Hint: you may fill in the blanks for what is more common for you: was a spouse unable to arrange pickup for your children at the last minute? Did a coworker fail to deliver their part of the project?*

**Your reframe**:

Now, take a few minutes to identify a situation that has been causing you grief — consider choosing something that seems to occur often. Use the Trifecta of Telling Yourself a Better Story to reframe the situation, and then answer the questions that follow. Remember, writing your responses is to help you get started, but the more you reframe in the moment, the easier and more automatic it will become. Soon you will not need to think about it at all, just like my experience with battle breathing.

**Situation:**

**Default Response:**

**Reframe:**

### What is actionable about your reframe?

### What is positive about your reframe?

### What is reality-based about your reframe?

## (8.6)
# STEP 6: REPEAT

*If you take just a handful* of learnings away from this book, I hope that this is one of them: *it's a numbers game*. For this Blueprint to work, replication is essential. The more positivity you can inject into your life, the better your life will be. The goal for you should be to repeat this process until it begins to happen automatically on a subconscious level — and it will. It is only a matter of time and repetition. Fasttrack your success by using every opportunity to tell yourself a better story; leverage every daily minor inconvenience at your disposal. Racking up a high score on easy mode will make it much easier for you to reframe the big stuff when it comes your way.

How will you know that the Blueprint is working? One way is to leverage the Positive and Negative Emotion Inventory assessment in the Establishing a Baseline chapter. You should notice your positive emotions on the rise and your negative ones declining. Another way to tell if the Blueprint is working is if you feel like you have more energy and mental resources at your disposal. If you find yourself smiling and laughing more, that is the Blueprint working. If you can meet criticism and adversity calmer and with more poise than before, you can be sure your efforts have been successful. Feeling safe and at peace are wonderful indicators that you are also on the right track. When you find meaningful solutions to your problems and feel more connected than ever to the people you care about, you will know the Blueprint is working for you.

Professor Fredrickson points out that over a three-month period, every cell in your body has died and been replaced, including neurons. In other words, every three months you are biologically a new you. If you can commit to this process for at least a three-month period, the chances of you creating a default preference for positivity are stacked wildly in your favor.

What is three months compared to the length of the rest of your hopefully very long life? Make it so!

# (9)
# BEST PRACTICES

*Best practices complement* any good process and give you additional tools and guidance to remain versatile. Investing time and effort into applying these best practices will reinforce the effectiveness of your daily efforts to reframe negative thought patterns into positive patterns for a broader and more beautiful life.

This list of best practices is lengthy, so I encourage you to mix-and-match the ones that that speak most strongly to you. Consider it a menu of sorts, so choose what is most appetizing to your mind. Feel good about the practices you can adopt and give yourself grace if you find the others are not as easily achieved. At the end of this chapter, you will be invited to identify three to five best practices you would like to implement in your life right away. As you read, create a mental shortlist of the most appealing practices to record in the Practical Application section.

Remember that achieving meaningful change is not about speed, rather than effort and recurrence. Just like the Blueprint, these practices will become easier over time with regular repetition.

Here is a categorized summary list for quick reference:

## BUILD SELF-AWARENESS
1. Know the Significance of Your Early Childhood
2. Reconnect With Your Childhood
3. Prioritize Your Life
4. Perform a Life Audit
5. Upgrade Your Vocabulary
6. Be Nice to Yourself
7. Count Your Blessings, Not Your Curses

## BRAIN & BODY HEALTH
8. Mind Your Mental Meals
9. Try New Things
10. Daily Stretching
11. Meditation
12. Prioritize Quality Sleep
13. Stay Hydrated
14. Spend Time in Nature
15. Enrich Your Environment

## STRENGTH IN COMMUNITIES
16. Do the Math
17. Connect With Yourself & Others
18. Give Back, Help Others, Contribute
19. Find Your Passion Project

## 1. Know the Significance of Your Early Childhood

The core personality of who you are today was formed between the ages of zero to seven years old. By the age of 10, most of your brain's physical structures have been formed. During adolescence, starting as early as 12 and going into the late teens, the brain undergoes a comprehensive pruning and reorganization process (the fact that teenage brains are "under heavy maintenance" demystifies teenagers in many ways). The brain will delete what is believed to be irrelevant information, solidifies well-established beliefs and patterns, and hard-codes associations gathered over the first decade of your life — whether they accurately reflect reality or not. The end result is the foundation of your mental and cognitive functions that you will build upon for the rest of your life.

What this means is that if you have not made a conscious effort to update your programming, you may very well be a 7-to-12-year-old walking around in an adult's body. When you apply this knowledge to other people in your life, does it help you make sense of their behaviors and beliefs? As with homes, if a foundation is faulty, it will need to be addressed for the rest of the house to remain sturdy and able to withstand the test of time.

As children, we are constantly experiencing, exploring, and integrating the stimulus that occurs all around us. We make associations based on cause-and-effect observations. When you're too young to feed yourself, you become cranky when hungry. When someone feeds you and you feel better, it becomes possible for you to associate your crankiness with being hungry. If, however, your caregiver was not attentive and punished you when you were cranky because of hunger, then you have a kind of disorganized association that does not meet your actual needs.

How might this disorganization be carried into adulthood? Perhaps when you feel hungry you snap at people, lashing out and feeling justified in doing so. If no one is around who can suggest you eat a Snickers, this behavior will continue until you fill the unmet need of being hungry. The (not so) technical term of this is "Hangry." As unpleasant as this condition is, it represents your disorganized communication between your subconscious and conscious minds. Once you can identify this, you can begin the work of creating a new communication method. This example is a simple one, with a simple driver — hunger. Imagine how much more complicated your communication style is when more complex emotions are involved linked to things like loneliness, love, perfection, insecurity, safety, or belonging.

The more disorganized your childhood, the more challenging your later years will be. This is why it is so important to understand not just the significance of childhood, but the significance of your *specific* childhood. While disorganization in your early childhood can be a setback, it is entirely possible to overcome through the power of self-awareness and neuroplasticity.

During our early childhoods, we are also inheriting the beliefs of our caregivers: parents, teachers, family members, even older siblings. We tend to take these things at face value and do not question their validity. For all of us, our first experiences are our normal, and we do not question our version of what is normal until forced to when exposed to other's beliefs.

It is not uncommon for people to *never* question the validity of their beliefs, but as part of this best practice I am asking you to do just that. By questioning your beliefs, their origins, and their application to your current adult life, you can begin to make choices about which beliefs serve you and should remain, and which should be retired.

## 2. Reconnect With Your Childhood

Reconnecting with your childhood is a way to nourish your inner child, the kiddo that is still very much a part of you. In my case, my inner child still enjoys squatting down and watching ant hills for what most people probably think is an excessive amount of time. Think about all the things you loved doing as a kid: cannonballs in the pool, craft nights, hide-and-seek, school-yard games, movie night, making forts, being silly, playing with Legos, coloring

— the list is infinite. Find ways to incorporate these things into your everyday adult life.

Why? Because it's a numbers game. You as a child had a default mode of happiness; all kids know how to enjoy themselves and live in the present moment. By taking inspiration from when you were in your purest form, you're able to inject more personal positivity into your life and help reinforce the commitment you made to your subconscious that you want to fill your days with positivity.

In short, we have a lot to re-learn from our inner child, and the reward for indulging in the things that made us happy as children is a deep and satisfying feeling of joy as adults.

## 3. Prioritize Your Life

What are the things you care about most in life? If you wrote down a list, and then compared it to where you spend the majority of your energy, do you think the two would be in balance? If, for example, you said spending time with family is your highest priority, but you are constantly working overtime and spend weekends exclusively catching up on chores or sleeping because of how tired you are … you are not in alignment with your actual priorities.

You may be thinking, "But, I work all those hours for the benefit of my family. What alternative is there?" And that is a valid sentiment to have. I don't know what the answer is in your situation — only you can know that — and developing a preference for positivity will help you come up with that answer. Remember, positivity helps you to be a better problem solver, and if time with your family is your highest priority, you can find a way to ensure you honor that priority. This could come in the form of a dedicated family game night, ensuring you are often available for a shared breakfast, performing small acts of kindness like leaving short notes or treats for your loved ones when you cannot be home.

The act of writing down your life's priorities is a steppingstone for achieving alignment with those priorities. It is a clear declaration to your conscious and subconscious mind of where you want to spend your time and energy. When you notice yourself giving preference to something other than a stated priority, pause and see if there is a way you can shift your trajectory to be more in line with your priorities.

This best practice is designed to help you achieve what is most important to you — not to society, or other people in your life — to *you*. When you live in accordance with your own priorities, you are creating a continuity that makes it much easier to maintain a preference for positivity.

One of the areas I committed to prioritizing in my life is quality time with my family — in large part due to the acknowledgement that change and loss can come around the corner at break-neck speed. This is what led to a two-month-long working road trip over the summer of 2023, which you will hear more about in the Benefits, Part 2 chapter.

## 4. Perform a Life Audit

In complement with the Prioritize Your Life best practice, performing an audit of your life will help you proactively address pain points that lead to negative thoughts or feelings. For example, if your sleep has been poor, take a moment to examine what could be contributing. Are the curtains not thick enough to keep out the glaring morning light, keeping you from sleeping until your alarm goes off? Is your pillow too thin or too thick? Are you being woken up when your partner needs to use the bathroom at night because they must turn on a light? Identifying what obstacles are present gives you the opportunity to address them; something as simple as a fresh pillow and different lighting options in your bedroom can lead to a drastic increase in the quality of your life. These little things add up, so examine as much of your life and the pain points that lurk in the shadows as possible.

Examples of pain points in life include long and unpleasant commutes, delayed but necessary home repairs, uncomfortable shoes leading to back or foot pain, trouble communicating with family members, challenging neighbors — the list goes on. Chances are some if not all these things have solutions or can be mitigated to be made less unpleasant and more tolerable overall.

I have been guilty over the years of simply suffering rather than trying to alleviate causes. During COVID, I began to experience more back pain than usual, which was making me irritable and generally unpleasant. After performing an audit, I pin-pointed all the contributing factors: my bed was not supportive enough, my computer chair not ergonomically correct, and my couch angle to the TV was all wrong. One at a time, I began to replace the troublesome furniture and found immediate relief. Old Adam would have suffered through the pain, not having the mental resources to connect the dots with my larger surroundings.

Since adopting a preference for positivity, solutions flow easily for my own challenges but also the challenges I see in others and the world. While you are developing your own preference for positivity, taking an audit of the pain points in your life will give you a clear idea of where to begin improving your life.

## 5. Upgrade Your Vocabulary

The words you use every day are the programming language that your brain uses to conduct its array of functions. Negative words reinforce to your subconscious that you prefer negativity and wish to seek it out. Positive words do the inverse.

When someone asks you, "How are you?" my guess is that your answer is like mine used to be: "Fine." "Good." "Okay."

What is preventing you from answering instead with, "Fantastic!" "Phenomenal!" or "Excellent!"?

This was a change I made after receiving advice from Aunt Ada, who seemed to have a vast amount of positive energy to pull from and an army of friends and supporters to show for it. When I adopted this practice, I didn't always feel "fantastic" — but it didn't take long for it to become true. What helped me along the way was seeing the surprise and delight on strangers' faces upon hearing my answer. The best way I can describe it is a kind of "awakening" from the autopilot they themselves were operating with, as if I had startled them awake from an unpleasant nap.

Not only was I boosting my own mood with this particular word choice, I was boosting theirs, too.

There are many other ways you can upgrade your vocabulary, like finding positive or affirming ways to say what you'd like to convey. Avoid words associated with negativity. Here is an example of what you might typically say, and what you can say instead:

"That was a weird experience." -> "That was a different experience." Or "That was a unique experience."

In this example, "weird" can have a negative connotation, whereas "different" is neutral and "unique" more positive. The meaning is essentially the same but the ways in which your brain will encode your observation will be positive rather than negative.

Also be sure to look out for negations. Your brain tends to edit out words like "not," "don't," "no," etc. and focus on what it actually hears. So, when you say:

"I don't want to eat junk food."

It edits out the "don't" and hears, "I want to eat junk food." This is because there are many alternatives to junk food, but you did not give your subconscious any direct alternative. All it heard was junk food, and so going forward it will draw your attention to chips, candies, crackers, and other delicious salty and sweet food because it believes that is what you want. Consider rephrasing statements like this to be more like:

"I want to eat more apples." "I want to only eat between 8 a.m. and 7 p.m." or "I'd like to experiment with more Mediterranean foods."

The intentional use of your words can go a long way towards reprogramming your thought patterns, which is why this best practice is an excellent supplement to the Blueprint to Happy process.

## 6. Be Nice To Yourself

Being nice to yourself is a combination of self-care, self-talk, and self-compassion. Together, they make up the framework for flourishing and do not require an external trigger. Rather, this becomes a simple state of being.

Self-care, self-talk, and self-compassion are things you can do every day that will set the conditions for happiness above and beyond following the Blueprint. They are the things that allow you to feel comfortable and secure in yourself so that you may share the excess energy and compassion created by being nice to yourself with others.

Self-care can range anywhere from things like brushing your teeth and grooming every day to ensuring that you get the restorative time and space you need to recover from difficult or stressful situations. It means paying attention to what you put into your body and keeping that body active and moving. Self-care means ensuring that you have the resources available to keep yourself stable and centered before giving any of your resources to others. It is a prioritization of self, because without your needs being cared for, what you can offer to others will be watered down and ineffective in the long term. In extreme circumstances, a lack of self-care can lead to a premature disablement or death that will leave your loved ones with nothing at all.

It is important to not confuse self-care with selfishness, where you put your desires above that of anyone else in your life. Selfishness is about *wants*, and self-care is about *needs*.

Self-talk means carefully choosing the words you use to talk to yourself, as well as the tone in which you use to think them. Are you hyper critical of yourself at every turn, using harsh and unforgiving language? Do you reinforce impossible standards by using absolutist language? Being nice to yourself in the context of self-talk is quite literal: go easy on your internal dialogs. Practice a kind and compassionate tone that you'd reserve for someone you love dearly. Loving yourself as dearly as your closest friend, partner, or child is the key to successful self-talk.

Self-compassion is the act of giving yourself grace no matter what the situation, and *especially* in situations where you have made mistakes or things did not go your way. Understanding that the past cannot be changed and moving forward with forgiveness will broaden your ability to make better choices going forward. Instead of being absorbed with anxiety, you will be capable of learning from the situation. Being critical of yourself may only serve to close your mind or avoid growing altogether. Compassion requires acceptance, which will be easier to accomplish when you embrace the binary view on control. When it becomes clear what you cannot control, radical acceptance becomes more accessible. Controlling how you treat yourself becomes the primary focus, and if the outcome will not change no matter what you do, I would rather smile than cry.

Finally, a wonderful daily practice you can adopt that will enable this best practice is to smile at yourself in the mirror when you find yourself in front of one. Smile as if you are greeting a trusted and close friend. This practice is right out of the playbook of Aunt Ada — she shared with me that this practice saw her through a tough time in her life when not many people were smiling around her. Remember that through self-compassion, you will always have a friendly face to greet you.

## 7. Count Your Blessings, Not Your Curses

Because the Blueprint to Happy is a numbers game, it will be important to focus on the positive things that happen to you daily rather than the negative. There are many creative ways to build this into your routine; my aunt has a "gratitude cup" where she writes down moments that made her happy or brought her joy and stores them in the cup. At the end of the year, she takes them out and reads them as part of a new year's ritual. Aim to be like Ada, who frequently needs to upsize her cup.

Others have told me they keep gratitude journals and make it a daily practice to write in them. A practice as simple as closing your eyes and listing things big and small that you are grateful for even for a short period of time — 30 seconds — will go a long way towards building a preference for positivity.

When doing daily gratitude exercises, it is important that each thing you list is different than the day before. You may be grateful for things that are not happening to you, such as the fact you do not live in a war zone. They can be small things, like a comfortable seat or clean air to breathe. The goal is to keep it fresh, so your brain doesn't get used to the pattern and then become blind to these gratefulness practices as just part of a rote routine.

Finally, pay attention to what you relay when someone asks how your day was. Do you immediately tell people what bothered you that day? Or what inconvenience or bad thing happened to you? If so, start counting your blessings instead of your curses. Start telling people about all the good stuff that happened to you; not only will this help to boost your mood, but it will also help to boost theirs as well. People will prefer your company over those who start with the laundry list of negatives.

## 8. Mind Your Mental Meals

As mentioned, your subconscious is busily taking in 11 million bits of data per second, which means that everything from the background chatter at the bar you're hanging out at, to the TV shows you fall asleep to are being dutifully processed by the supercomputer that runs most of your life. Your subconscious adds this input to the data warehouse and uses it to interpret your preferences. If true crime is your go-to entertainment preference, your subconscious is probably going to be more likely to bring to your attention all the negative news about real life tragedies. It will ignore the feel-good humanitarian stories, or even the positive things that are happening for you in favor of giving you more of what it thinks you want.

One of the best choices I have made in recent years is cancelling my cable subscription, which effectively severed the addiction I had formed to cable news. It took a lot longer than I care to admit, but once it was no longer an option for me to flip on the news during lunch breaks and after work, my already pretty great life increased in quality tenfold.

One of the things that helped me take the leap was learning about a study that showed, on average, people who watch the news overestimate the amount of crime occurring at any given time. People who did not watch as much or consumed no news at all were much closer in their estimation of actual crime rates. This once again highlights how the negativity bias drives news cycles and what we pay attention to when we watch the news.

I found myself having to make intentional decisions about what I was putting in my brain. Instead of the news, I turned to educational content, content that stimulated my mind and continued to build on the skills that were spring boarding me to a happier life. I got my news via public radio, re-started reading half-finished books and found myself more likely to play and enjoy vinyl records in their entirety. I came to realize that I really enjoyed soaking in the sounds of a full album, the experience intended by the artist.

If nothing else, keep in mind that your subconscious is always alert and listening, even when you are sleeping. It is the part of the brain that wakes you up when it senses something amiss. If you are one to sleep with the TV on, consider what plays all night long: infomercials and reruns. Is this the kind of content you wish to fill your data warehouse with?

## 9. Try New Things

The Blueprint to Happy relies on your brain's ability to rewire itself through intentional repetition. The brain is perfectly capable of making changes, however its efficiency and speed in doing so will vary by person. The good news is that you can increase your brain's ability to make new connections by trying new things. Exposing yourself to novel experiences encourages neuroplasticity, which is the brain's ability to create new connectors and to repurpose existing connections.

It is therefore a best practice to find new things to try — if not daily than at least weekly. Try out a new venue, take a walk in a new park or a different part of town you haven't checked out yet. Learn a new game, or pick up new words from a different language. Consider cooking new dishes, or trying new foods in general. When grocery shopping, challenge yourself to purchase a new food to try for the first time. The international aisle is a great place to begin this ritual. Watch something different, and invest some of your time in becoming a constant learner. What you learn is up to you: If you like to draw, learn new techniques. If you are into cars, learn about the cutting-edge automobile technology that is being developed. Read books in different genres than you are used to.

The possibilities are endless, and the benefits are tangible. By combining the trying of new things with the Blueprint to Happy, you are fast-tracking your success in creating positive thought patterns while becoming more experienced and attractive to others. This will increase your influence, which is the most valuable currency in our human society. Finally, trying new things gives you more potential overlap with new and existing friends, partners, and family members. This will deepen your relationships which carries with it the benefits of security — which we all desire — through connectedness.

## 10. Daily Stretching

Stretching daily is a great way to check in with your body: where are you tight, where are you the most tender? Chances are, these are the places where you hold your stress the most. By stretching them out daily, you are creating a positive mind-body connection, and giving yourself information so that as you go through your day you can pay better attention to which parts of your body are tensing and under what circumstances it occurs. This will help you with the Notice step of the Blueprint, and continuing the activity daily will help you notice if you transferred one area of tightness to another.

In addition to these factors, stretching — especially before bedtime — has been shown to contribute to better sleep quality, as well as to increase overall blood circulation. Because of the increase in blood circulation, your muscles are getting more oxygen which flushes out metabolic waste products. In short, stretching will make you feel better, and feeling better goes a long way towards happiness. It is tough to look for the positive if you are struggling with chronic pain, and daily stretching is one way to lower your pain levels or prevent chronic pain from forming in the first place.

Don't think you have enough time in your day to stretch? Call upon the Life Audit best practice and audit your day. Can you stretch while you wait for coffee to perk? Can you clear a space on your floor and stretch while you watch your favorite program? Even five minutes a day adds up to 35 minutes a week, which is more than two hours of stretching every month.

## 11. Meditation

Meditation can be an intimidating prospect for many who are unfamiliar with the practice, or think they are simply not capable because of racing thoughts or general inexperience. The good news about meditation is that any amount — even 30 seconds worth — has tremendous benefits for your mind. If you are only able to meditate for a short time, that's okay. Just keep going; as time goes on it will get easier and eventually you'll find yourself craving it.

Meditation is also a wonderful tool to help bring your conscious and subconscious minds into alignment. We talked about the subconscious mind being like a supercomputer, taking in millions of data bits per second all day and night long. Meditation creates a space where your conscious mind can open, and with the help of the subconscious mind, connect dots in your experiences or thoughts that can be deeply meaningful and helpful in your day-to-day life. One of my favorite ways to solve problems in my life is to share with my subconscious what I want to solve, and then consciously forget about it for a day or more. During my meditation sessions, answers to these problems often flow — my supercomputer has done all the calculations subconsciously. I sometimes think of this as a "brain download," and look forward to getting a seemingly random bolt of insight after tasking my subconscious with solving a problem for me. This kind of teamwork between you and your subconscious has limitless possibilities.

Here is a very simple way to start — give it a try after reading and assess how you feel both before and after.

Sit comfortably so that your feet are flat on the floor, and your back is straight. Close your eyes, and inhale deeply in through your nose, and exhale through your mouth. Continue breathing like this for a few more breaths and then imagine roots growing from the soles of your feet into the floor. Imagine them growing in length down into the earth, very deep, all the way to the core of the earth. Once you feel connected through your feet, imagine a white beam of light coming from the crown of your head, reaching into the sky like a beacon. Throughout the process, continue your deep breathing and allow your muscles to relax. Allow yourself to enjoy the sensation of being connected both above and below, and let your mind simply rest as peacefully as possible. You may also imagine all the negative energy within you expelled into the ground, and fresh, positive, and pure energy flowing into you from the beam at the crown of your head. When you are ready, open your eyes and continue with your day.

The reason meditation is helpful in your pursuit of happiness is because it is another tool to create a sense of psychological safety so your brain can work without the hyper vigilance it may otherwise be under. If you are able to meditate, you are signaling to your brain and your body that you are in a safe place where you can allow your mind to be at ease.

Meditation is a time where your mind is not working overtime to manage memories of the past or worries about the future; meditation is all about being in the present moment. This gives your brain more time to check in with the body and strive towards homeostasis.

## 12. Prioritize Quality Sleep

When you sleep, your brain undergoes a cleansing process required to maintain healthy cognitive functions. When you are in a deep sleep, the glymphatic system flushes the brain with fluids, which clears out the waste from your waking hours. Waste occurs because your body's cells, including in the brain, are constantly dying and being replaced. The dead cells need to be flushed from your body, otherwise they will build up and cause health complications. The waste leaves through your bloodstream and eventually exits your body by way of the bladder.

Because this process typically occurs during deep sleep, denying yourself quality sleep puts you at major risk for reduced brain function. If you are consistently short-changing yourself from a sleep perspective, and the neglect goes on for too long, the waste in your brain can lead to decreases in cognition, decline in memory, and conditions as serious as dementia.

Quality sleep is something you should avoid compromising on if you wish to have a vibrant intellectual life well into your old age. It is a best practice for the Blueprint because we're relying on the robust functions of your brain to rewire your preferences. If you're sleep deprived, it will make the process much more difficult to follow.

To help yourself get consistently good sleep, try setting a regular sleep and wake time for all seven days of the week. Consider creating a pre-sleep routine that primes your brain and body to relax and ready themselves for sleep. Remember that your brain likes being able to predict what will happen and when, and sleep is no different. My sleep shutdown process usually looks like this: listen to music while I stretch and then shower, brush teeth, meditate (if I have time), and then settle in for sleep. I do all of this within my bedroom, associating all these activities with the process of sleep. Another tip is to avoid using your bed as a "catch-all" where you eat, watch programs, browse on your phone, read books, etc. Using your bed for more than sleeping confuses the brain and it will be less likely to cooperate when it comes to getting quality sleep.

## 13. Stay Hydrated

For similar reasons as prioritizing quality sleep, it is important to stay hydrated to attain peak brain performance. Your brain is suspended in fluid relational to how much water you drink, and the amount of fluid present is directly correlated with brain function. The water levels in your body assist in clearing out toxins and waste, as well as in carrying nutrients to the brain. Becoming dehydrated can lead to lower levels of brain function, memory loss, and has even been linked to feelings of anxiety, dejection, and irritability. In addition to your brain, the rest of your body and organs rely on water for healthy functioning. Your immune system has an easier time navigating your body when it is well hydrated, which is why all doctors recommend drinking plenty of fluids when sick. So why not preempt sickness by just being hydrated all the time?

Avoid brain fog by drinking enough water. Consider making a commitment to start your day by drinking a tall glass of cold or room temperature water, depending on your preference. Giving your organs a glass of water to start the day wakes them up and makes them very happy. This is an easy way to exercise self-care and set yourself up for success when it comes to executing the Blueprint to Happy.

## 14. Spend Time in Nature

In 2021, the National Center for Biotechnology Information published a review of a decade's worth of experimental and observational studies regarding the impacts of nature exposure on health.[4] They found "evidence for associations between nature exposure and improved cognitive function, brain activity, blood pressure, mental health, physical activity, and sleep. Results from experimental studies provide evidence of protective effects of exposure to natural environments on mental health outcomes and cognitive function."

The reason why nature has this impact on us is currently elusive, but we can say with a high degree of certainty there is a positive link. So why not take advantage of this knowledge and boost your chances of living a happier life by getting out into nature more often? This best practice is an easy way to supercharge your happiness journey — because it's a numbers game. Anything repeated will be logged as part of your overall preferences, so find ways to get nature into your everyday life for an easy win.

This doesn't mean you need to live next to a National Park or travel great distances to spend time in nature. Any green space will do; parks big and small will give you the nature experience required to realize the benefits of this best practice. If you have one, even sitting in your back yard and bird watching will go a long way towards building tranquility in your mind, with the added bonus of lowering your blood pressure.

---

[4] Associations between Nature Exposure and Health: A Review of the Evidence, Published online 2021 Apr 30 https://www.ncbi.nlm.nih.gov/pmc/articles/PMC8125471/

Another option is to bring the outdoors indoors. There are studies that show healing in hospitals is quicker when windows with nature views are available.[5] Opening a window on a nice day, placing bird feeders within view, or having small nature mementos around to touch such as an acorn or flowers will go a long way. The act of opening curtains to let the sunshine in can make a huge difference in mood.

## 15. Enrich Your Environment or "Improve Your Cage"

A drug addiction study conducted in the 1970s called "Rat Park" gives us a window into how important our environments are to our overall mental health. Rat Park was a response to an earlier experiment where a solitary rat was put in a barren cage with the option of regular water or drug-laced water to drink. The solitary rat seemed to form a preference for the drug water, and then a dependency, and then suffered a fatal overdose from over-imbibing. Until the Rat Park experiment came around, this early study was taken to mean that drugs have an addictive and fatal quality.

Dr. Bruce Alexander was not satisfied with that conclusion, however, and wanted to know if it was the drug that was causing the addictive behavior, or the environment. So, he constructed Rat Park, a paradise for rats that included a large, multi-tiered cage, colorful toys, a variety of cheeses, and perhaps most importantly, other rats. He then introduced the regular water and the drug water to see if the original experiment's results would be replicated.

What happened next was the opposite of the original experiment. The rats in Rat Park largely ignored the drug water, and the rats who drank it did so recreationally and in moderation.

---

5  View through a window may influence recovery from surgery, Published April 1984 https://pubmed.ncbi.nlm.nih.gov/6143402/

This outcome radically challenged the conclusions of the previous study, finding that not only was the drug water not addictive, it also wasn't fatal. The main difference between the studies is clear: one had an enriched environment where addiction was avoided, while the baren environment resulted in fatal levels of addiction.

Addiction on a human level is something we might best associate with escapism. If you find yourself wanting to escape your life, the answer isn't drugs, social media, video games, etc. The answer is to enrich your environment with both pleasing stimulation and companionship.

Enriching your environment can include hanging pleasing art or family photographs around your house, apartment, or room. It can take the form of having a comfortable chair to sit in, or optimizing your kitchen so it is easy to use. Maybe it means creating more conversation spaces so you can have guests over for visits or adding houseplants to nurture and enjoy. Whatever you think will make it more enjoyable to inhabit your life, do it! Enrich your environment to help create another layer of safety and security in your life, so your mind knows it can rest easy and take care of your inner workings, including building that preference for positivity.

## 16. Do the Math

Think about your favorite person who doesn't share a residence with you. Maybe it is your mom, dad, brother, best friend, aunt, or cousin. How many more years will you have to enjoy their company? Within a single year, how many actual times will you see them? If your favorite person is your mom who lives in another state, will you only see her for holidays and maybe birthdays? Two or three times a year over 10 years is only 20 or 30 visits *total*.

Oftentimes we can fall into the trap of feeling like we have infinite time with the people we love, and eventually get whacked in the face with the truth. My appeal to you is to not wait until that happens and make the most of the time you have with people now, in the present moment. Do the math and see how much time you really have left with the important people in your life. Use that knowledge as motivation to make every minute and hour count.

On a personal note, COVID was the catalyst for me to prioritize more time with my friends and family, and I am glad that I have. Before the pandemic, I would hear of the occasional death impacting my friends and coworkers, but since 2020, it is hard to say just how many times I have expressed my condolences for someone's untimely loss. My family has seen a number of losses to premature deaths over the past three years. The truth is that so many have been exposed to a new virus we still do not fully understand. What we do understand is that the coronavirus attacks organs, weakening them and making worse any pre-existing conditions people may have otherwise had managed before becoming infected. I believe there is still a lot of loss to come our way from the resulting complications which we cannot control. What we can control is how we choose to prioritize our time and commitments. I urge you to consider this factor as you prioritize your life and do the math.

## 17. Connect With Yourself & Others

Following from the findings of Rat Park, another best practice is to connect with yourself so you can make better and more meaningful connections with others. By working through the process of the Blueprint to Happy, you are already going to learn more things about yourself and what you truly care about. Use these learnings to seek connections with others who are likely to share your values, goals, and overall energy.

In extreme circumstances like trauma healing, community has

been shown to be one of the key components to recovery. Human beings evolved as a social species, and the hormones that are released as part of a stress response like oxytocin are designed to prompt you to seek out others for help, comfort, or both.

Having a community that you know you can rely on and that you also contribute to increases the amount of psychological safety you have at your disposal. As we've discussed, feeling safe is an essential component of being able to think clearly and broadly. The more secure we are about the people we have in our lives, the better our cognition, problem solving, and capacity for positivity will be.

## 18. Give Back, Help Others, Contribute

Purpose is a fuel for the spirit that seems to have no limitations. A person filled with purpose can do anything. People often struggle to find purpose, and therefore struggle to get by, to see a point of the life they are living. One way to feel purposeful is to give back, help others, or contribute in some meaningful way to the whole. Another way you can think about this is as selfless action, be it helping out a family member who can never repay you, volunteering locally, youth mentoring, or driving social change. The list is infinite, as there is no shortage in this world of people who could use help and compassion.

Where people tend to get hung up when it comes to helping others is either a lack of time, lack of energy, or both. If you lack time, focus on something small you can do until you have more

> "The ideal person enjoys doing small favors for others."
> — Aristotle

time to dedicate to a cause you really care about. Something that isn't simply a monetary donation; it is best if you can look into the eyes of someone you are helping, and especially to see their smiles. This could be as easy as making it a point to hold doors open for people, share a genuine complement, or uplift people with your own positive energy, and maybe even a good-humored joke.

Since being home more because of COVID, I take walks around my neighborhood as often as possible. Early on, I noticed the trash near the road that had either escaped the garbage collection effort or had been left by less mindful folks. This was not a new occurrence; after ten years of living in the neighborhood I noticed trash showing up in my yard from time to time. For longer than I am happy to admit, my mindset was "someone should do something about that." Right up until I realized, "Hey, I'm someone."

So, I decided to combine my walk with this best practice and began picking up trash along my usual route. Because trash is gross, I invested in gloves, a grabber stick, and a trash can with a sling so I could still comfortably enjoy my walk. It didn't take long for neighbors to notice — many waved appreciatively or made a point to say "thank you" directly for what I was doing. Sometimes my cat Lucy — a calico that showed up at my doorstep a decade ago when I bought my house — would walk along with me on these trash pickup adventures. Well, at least to the edge of her cat-territory before going back to wait for me by the house. The result of this small act of kindness was not only a boost in my own mood, but that of my neighbors who could see that they lived in a community where someone cared to contribute to the betterment of the neighborhood instead of just themselves.

If you lack the energy, then this is a best practice you can come back to after the Blueprint to Happy has restored a sense of security within you to the point that your energy has returned. You may be surprised to find out how much energy helping others will give you in the end; these moments of contributing to the happiness and wellbeing of others may just be what helps you get through a rough patch or overcome the self-doubt that visits even the happiest of people.

## 19. Find Your Passion Project

There are times in life where we seem to have access to a wellspring of energy and enthusiasm. The easiest examples to point to are when we are actively falling in love or are engaged in some creative pursuit that seems to touch our mind, body, and spirit. In these moments, it might feel like you can stay up for days, or that you can't wait to get out of bed to get back to enjoying these things in your life. Eventually these feelings wane because of one reason or another: you get used to your new relationship, you finish your creative project, you get distracted or interrupted or some unforeseen circumstance comes along to knock you off your axis.

Ask yourself: where does this wellspring of energy and enthusiasm come from? The answer is you. This comes from a place inside of you that is, in fact, accessible at *any* time.

One way to reliably access it is to have a passion project — something that cannot be completed in a week's time, but perhaps would benefit from a *lifetime's* worth of work on your part. Pace yourself so that you don't get burned out but stay engaged enough to access this wellspring of energy on a daily, weekly, or monthly basis.

A passion project is all about what *you* are passionate about: perhaps it is outreach to the unhomed, early childhood education, addiction recovery, childhood access to sports or music, trauma healing, community works — the list is literally endless. What calls to you will always benefit from your help, and your helping others will always help you.

> **"Have a dream so big that you cannot achieve it until you grow into the person who can."**
> — Unknown

In his published reflections titled *Man's Search for Meaning* on his experiences during World War II as a prison camp and Holocaust survivor, Viktor Frankl explains the main difference between those who survived the horrors of work camps and those who did not was the sense of purpose. If a person believed that their life had a purpose, their ability to hold on and see themselves through the war was much greater. He reported that those who no longer felt that life held any purpose for them died within days, or even hours of voicing this belief.

Purpose can see people through the worst horrors of our existence. If that is true for WWII survivors, imagine what is possible for people who find their purpose and passion free of great strife, violence, and oppression.

**PRACTICAL APPLICATION #11**

Take a few moments to reflect on all the best practices, and then choose three to five that are most appetizing to you. Write down which ones appealed to you most in the left-hand column of the table below. In the right-hand column, jot down some notes about how you could fit this practice into your life, and how it will feel when you do.

| # | Best Practice | How will this fit into your life? How will it feel? |
|---|---|---|
| 1 | | |
| 2 | | |

## (10)

# MANTRAS AND MAXIMS TO LIVE BY

*Mantras and maxims* are intended to be bite-sized morsels of wisdom that contain big ideas in the smallest number of words possible. They are short for the sake of efficiency, making them easy to deploy as reminders of deep knowledge in the short span of time it takes to regroup during a stressful meeting or chaotic family outing. They help you return to your center, stay true to your path, and maintain your brain's preference for positivity.

Consider these your starter list, and I encourage you to seek out your own as you traverse your life's journey. These concentrated doses of wisdom can make all the difference when you don't have the time or resources to do a complete reframe in the moment. Collect and use them like another tool in your kit to build your best possible life.

### 100% of zero is zero

I use this saying to remind myself that if I do not take care of my own needs, even though I may want to help others, that effort will ultimately fail, because 100% of nothing is still nothing. If I have depleted myself emotionally or physically, that means I have nothing to give others, even if I wanted to. When I talk to struggling moms who are putting their family needs above their own for long and sustained periods of time, I will often share this saying. The same goes for stressed-out managers who are trying to take care of everyone and everything else before themselves. 100% of zero is zero.

## Growing pains mean that you are growing

This saying serves me when I find myself fearful of trying something new or taking a risk. It is an acknowledgement that while there may be pain along the way, the pain will grow me. I will become stronger and more confident because of it, because growing pains mean that you are growing.

## When the outcome will remain the same no matter what I do, I'd rather smile than cry

A variation of the advice not to cry over spilled milk, this saying is an acknowledgement of what is outside of my control. It is also a reinforcement that I have a choice in how I respond to all that is uncontrollable; if my reaction is really all that I have control over, it is an empowering experience to choose to smile.

In the Bhagavad Gita, Lord Krishna avails that when we are the same in sorrow as we are in happiness, we have attained a divine state. I can say from personal experience that it indeed feels divine to meet the moment with a smile, especially when it is a difficult moment.

## When you ask the universe for something, make sure it has a way to give it to you

If you want to win the lottery, buying a lottery ticket is a requirement. If you have goals in life, this saying will remind you to think about what you are doing to make those goals achievable. Are you setting the conditions for success? If you wish to be more connected for your profession, are you actively attending networking engagements? If you know you have unresolved trauma or emotional challenges, have you taken the time to find a professional and attend therapy?

In my experience, the universe is eager to help you accomplish your goals, but it cannot help if you do not do your part in opening doors and creating entrances to see your wishes fulfilled.

## Your brain believes what you tell it to believe

I use this saying when doubts sneak in about my ability to change my own mindset or worldview. If negative thoughts are making their way through, this is how I galvanize my resolve in telling myself a better story.

## The best time to plant a tree is 20 years ago; the second best time is now

Derived from an ancient Chinese proverb, the message here is that we should not let a delayed action stop us from taking action altogether. If something was important and impactful in the past, chances are it is still important and impactful in the present. We cannot know the future, but we can influence it with our present actions. Delaying an action further because you already missed the opportunity once is a great way to languish and a breeding ground for more delays.

## Don't suffer twice when once is enough

When we worry about something that *might* happen, you are suffering preemptively. If what you are worried about comes to be, you will have suffered twice. Instead, take things as they come and avoid unnecessary suffering — once is enough, why sign up for more? I have heard this referred to as "anticipatory anxiety," which has an interesting cure in the discipline of logotherapy.[6] If, for example, you are worried about sweating through your clothes during a presentation, you can joke with yourself about *how much* you will sweat. In doing this, you're taking the fear factor out of your anticipatory anxiety which is what usually makes what you are worrying about into a self-fulfilling prophesy. Also see the maxim: "What you resist, persists."

## Pay attention to what you are resisting — that is where your growth potential is

This maxim is a nod to the Notice and Investigate steps in the Blueprint. Resistance is an indicator that we are feeling unsafe about a course of action, and figuring out why you feel resistant will allow you to tell yourself a better story so you can dissipate the resistance and move forward. The result is growth from surviving something you may have considered scary or intimidating. You will find your capabilities expanding, and the more you perform this audit on what you resist, the more you will be able to grow your capabilities. The complementary maxim, "What you resist, persists," is a warning that ignoring something does not actually make it go away.

---

6 *Man's Search for Meaning* by Viktor Frankl, published by Beacon Press 1959, Logotherapy as a Technique

## Healthy positivity means acknowledging the negative while making a commitment to not be controlled by it

We live in a world that is as vast as it is nuanced, and there is real evil, corruption, tragedy, and suffering out there. This book and the practices within are not an attempt to deny this reality. Rather, it is an appeal that we should not allow ourselves to be controlled by the negative forces of the world and life. It is a far greater positive impact to the world if we can show up with kindness and empathy in our hearts as much as possible. In this way, we can be the bright guiding light of an alternative way of being, giving those in the grips of negativity an opportunity to choose another path.

## What you tolerate becomes your standard

Because our subconscious will steer us towards what is familiar — regardless of whether it is good for us or not — what you tolerate will become your every-day. For example, if you have a spouse that makes disparaging remarks that you do not like, but also simply put up with, you have allowed this behavior to be your standard. The message here is to not tolerate the things in life that drag you down, or before you know it they will seem normal and increasingly un-changeable.

It may be a good idea to look for what you are tolerating during your Life Audit best practice. Was there a lot of yelling in your household as a child, and as a result yelling has become acceptable in your adult life? Understanding the origins of what you tolerate will better help you assess if you wish to keep things as they are, or make a change that will contribute more towards your happiness.

## Change happens one person at a time; be a part of the change that makes us better as a whole

When people lament about how bad society has become, I like to ask them what part they are playing in making it better. When good people remove themselves from society through isolation or intentional non-engagement, of course society gets worse. We must ask ourselves what role we play in making the world we'd like to live in.

## The first step to getting the help you need is wanting the help you need

A lot of people may have a sense that they want their lives to improve, but do not actively seek help in making it happen. Perhaps like I once believed, they think that their lives are un-changeable, and they must simply suffer through their days accordingly. This maxim is a good reminder that if we need help, the first place to begin is by asking for it, be that by engaging friends and family, or a more formal approach like therapy or a life coach.

## Feeling safe is a requirement for healing

This saying is a reminder that we cannot heal if we do not feel safe. If healing is our top priority, we must first create conditions in which we feel safe enough to do so.

## "Show, don't tell" applies as much to life as it does to writing

When we tell someone that we love them over and over again, sometimes it can lose its meaning. If, however, we show someone we love them by doing small favors, asking about their day, caring about their health, making thoughtful plans to spend time with them, etc. we are *showing* our love instead of merely telling. Words can be powerful, but they gain their most power when they are paired with actions.

## Every step is a good one so long as it takes you even a millimeter closer to what you want

This saying reinforces the idea that there is no progress too small when we are making an effort to improve our lives or the lives of others. Millimeters added up over a lifetime can easily turn into kilometers, and sometimes the smaller steps are the best ones. It allows us to pace ourselves and avoid burnout. It might prevent us from getting too far along only to learn we had made a wrong turn sometime back.

## Practice makes progress

Continuing the theme of incremental progress, practice can be reliably counted on to get us closer to our goals. This can apply to anything ranging from meditation to painting. From conversational skills to physical fitness regimen. It certainly applies to the Blueprint: as you work towards reframing your thoughts in a meaningful and impactful way, progress will follow practice.

In this way, strive to be an active practitioner when it comes to your own happiness. That means practicing elements of the Blueprint as often as possible, until you are a master practitioner.

## Self-awareness is the first step towards self-acceptance

How can you accept something you don't fully understand? Until you know yourself, you cannot truly love yourself, and the lack of clarity will only add to feelings of mistrust and discomfort. Take a long and clear look at yourself, make it a regular practice, and love that person unconditionally. This combination of awareness and acceptance is jet fuel for the Blueprint's engine.

## Successfully modeling healthy and productive behaviors is the strongest form of influence

If you want to convince someone that something is a good idea, you have to show them what it looks like and what the results are. This is a maxim that has driven me to practice all of the techniques in the Blueprint regularly, as well as to actively live my values instead of just talking about them. If one of your goals is to have a positive influence on others, the most direct path to achieving that influence is to show them the way with your own actions and ensuring people can see a direct correlation between those actions and the positive results.

> "Example isn't another way to teach. It is the only way to teach."
> — Albert Einstein

Oftentimes when I hear people talk about how to solve the world's problems, they point to the need to teach children things like tolerance, climate change awareness, emotional intelligence, and so on. My counterpoint to this idea is that children learn by example, so to me it is far more important that adults adopt these learnings in a demonstratable way so that our children will grow up seeing them as normal and proper.

## The only guarantee in life is the present moment — make the most of it

COVID is what hammered this concept home for me, which I consider a gift that I intend to appreciate and enjoy for the rest of my life. At any given time, we could fall ill, or be impacted by unexpected tragedy. We may lose a treasured person in our lives, even when we thought we would have many more hours, days, months, or years with them. It is for this reason we must prioritize the important things in our lives and actively engage in them. If you are like me and spending time with family and friends is your priority, that means you say yes to invitations out, or holiday gatherings. It means you host your family members for extended stays and go on road trips to see as many people who are important to you as possible.

## Accusations are often confessions

This maxim is useful for reminding ourselves during times of conflict and interpersonal strife that what people often accuse us of doing are indicators of what they are struggling with. Understanding this opens the door to responding with empathy instead of outrage or denial. Much of the Blueprint is designed to help you achieve inner peace and security, which makes empathy much easier as you are no longer focused on your insecurities and can be more open to seeing someone else's situation. When people confess their struggles to you in this way, know that their accusation is not personal, and see if you can help them using this new insight they have given you.

## Everyone is the hero of their own story

Following on the previous maxim, it is important to know that each individual works from a place of good intentions — mostly for themselves. Sometimes our good intentions get turned sideways and go the other direction, but our perception of doing good or being good remains the same. Even people who have committed and been convicted of violent and harmful crimes will insist upon the goodness of their character. Hitler was the hero of his own story, as obviously terrible as he was. So, when you encounter people who have harmful behaviors for themselves or others, there is a good chance that they do not see the flaws in their approach. Similarly, you may not see the flaws in your approach as you navigate life, and even may be seen as the "villain" in someone else's story, despite your conviction that you fit the role of hero better.

This maxim is powerful because it gives us a necessary window into the human condition, allowing us to meet the moment with more empathy and introspection than we might have otherwise.

## Pessimism is a choice

Because I am human, I sometimes find myself leaning towards a pessimistic outlook, especially at times when I am exhausted, hungry, or out of my comfort zone. It is in these moments that I use this maxim to remind myself that my reaction to what is happening in life is a choice, and often the only choice that I have. The world contains a spectrum of truth; while negativity is real, so is positivity. What we choose to focus on is completely up to us, and the options are unlimited. Choose optimism.

## Being nice to yourself is the first step to being nice to anyone else

When you are struggling to find empathy and kindness to share with others, it may be a good idea to look inward and see how well you are sharing those qualities with yourself. You may find it more comfortable and possible to be kind and thoughtful towards others, but you will find yourself increasingly depleted and unable to extend kindness if you are withholding it from yourself. This maxim reminds us to apply the proverbial oxygen mask to ourselves before we try to help others do the same.

## (11)

# THE BLUEPRINT AND WEATHERING ADVERSITY

*Practicing the Blueprint to Happy* is admittedly much easier when you are in a real place of safety and security. In the situations where your mind is your greatest adversary and no other major forces are working against you, the Blueprint to Happy is a sure bet. That said, if the reason your thought patterns tend to be more negative is because you are in actual peril or struggling to meet your basic needs, following the Blueprint will undoubtedly be harder.

Harder, but not impossible.

First and foremost, your physical and mental safety should come first. No amount of positive thinking will solve for immediate danger, and you should correctly narrow your focus in order to create safe conditions as soon as possible. That said, for situations that are chronically challenging from a safety perspective, creating positive thought patterns instead of negative ones will make you much more likely to achieve a positive result that will serve your best interests.

I can think of no better example of this philosophy applied than a woman named Magda Hellinger, author of the book *The Nazi's Knew My Name: A Remarkable Story of Survival and Courage in Auschwitz*. Magda was a 25-year-old kindergarten teacher in Eastern Slovakia when she and over a hundred other young single women from her town were deported to Germany. They, among hundreds of others who they joined along the way, were the second wave of prisoners to arrive at the infamous Auschwitz concentration camp. Because she spoke German, Magda was forced into a leadership position by the Nazis, responsible for thousands of prisoners throughout her three years at Auschwitz.

Three years. Three years of living in squalor with disease, death, and torture around every single corner of existence.

Throughout her memoir, Magda recounts the mantra both she and others used in order to survive the horrors the Nazi's imposed upon them: to get through this, we must stick together. Using this mantra, Magda saved thousands of lives by outwitting and outmaneuvering her Nazi captors. She had to make hard choices and see many, many more sent to their deaths while she could do nothing. But she held to her mantra and survived for three long years, including the death march that preceded her liberation.

In these same years, she met her future husband who also survived the horrors of the Holocaust. They went on to make a life for themselves, ultimately moving to Australia and raising a loving family. It was her daughter who finally finished her memoir and published it posthumously.

I recount this amazing woman's life as an example of the power of thoughts; no other explanation can be had as to how this woman could survive the Nazis knowing her name. Her ability to keep her wits, problem solve, and bind her community together to simply *survive* derives from her power of thought. Her power of *positive* thought. She did not succumb to the very real despair all around her. She was not paralyzed by the injustice of what was happening to her. All throughout her story she makes sacrifices for others, giving her clothes, her food, her bravery in the face of evil so that others might have a chance of surviving.

Similarly, another Holocaust survivor Viktor Frankl speaks in his book *A Man's Search for Meaning* about the power of the internal world when it comes to facing adversity. Frankl was a trained psychiatrist at the time of his internment. He used his training and knowledge to help him survive his ordeal and sustained himself with a purpose: by surviving he could share his uniquely informed perspective and experience with the world after the war. He made efforts to clinically observe the circumstances, reactions, and experiences of those within the camp, himself included. He writes:

> "Is that theory true which would have us believe that man is no more than a product of many conditional and environmental factors – be they of a biological, psychological or sociological nature? Is man but an accidental product of these? Most important, do the prisoners' reactions to the singular world of the concentration camp prove that man cannot escape the influences of his surroundings? Does man have no choice in action in the face of such circumstances?
>
> We can answer these questions from experience as well as on principle. The experiences of camp life show that one does have a choice of action. There are enough examples, often of a heroic nature, which proved that apathy could be overcome, irritability

suppressed. Man *can* persevere a vestige of spiritual freedom, of independence of mind, even in such terrible conditions of psychic and physical stress.

We who lived in concentration camps can remember men who walked through the huts comforting others, giving away their last piece of bread. They may have been few in number, but they offer sufficient proof that everything can be taken from a man but one thing: the last of the human freedoms – to choose one's attitude in any given set of circumstances, to choose one's own way.

And there were always choices to make. Every day, every hour, offered the opportunity to make a decision, a decision which determined whether you would or would not submit to those powers which threatened to rob you of your very self, your inner freedom; which determined whether or not you would become the plaything of circumstance, renouncing freedom and dignity to become molded into the form of the typical inmate."

Frankl also describes how focusing his mind on the pleasant memories and thoughts of his wife very likely saved his sanity and his life as he worked in freezing conditions without adequate clothing or footwear.

Very real adversity and injustice are still a part of our world, which is why this book is being written. Governmental and institutional protections are increasingly failing — and they have never been a sure bet in the first place. The very same authority that is supposed to protect and serve can be turned around and wielded unjustly at breakneck speeds, as demonstrated to us by the Nazis. It is up to each individual to fortify their minds to meet the moment with as many mental resources available as possible. This preserves our ability to work together, to problem solve, and to see a light at the end of what seems like a very long tunnel.

It is worth noting that both Magda and Viktor lived long lives and were able to create nurturing family environments after their traumatic experience. Viktor Frankl was deported at the age of 37 and lived to the age of 92 — even after enduring three years of starvation conditions, hard labor, exposure to the elements, zero health care, and frequent disease outbreaks. After the war, he advocated against retaliation and mass guilt, knowing that such negative emotions were poisons rather than elixirs. If this is not an endorsement of healthier living through positive mindsets, I don't know what is.

People like Magda Hellinger and Viktor Frankl are not the first to build resiliency through a positive mindset, and they certainly won't be the last. Theirs are the most striking examples, but every single human on earth is capable of harnessing this power of positive thought.

At the end of the day, no one knows more about your unique situation than you do. Not only that, but you also possess a supercomputer designed to connect countless datapoints and arrive at solutions tailored for your exact needs. What gets in the way is negativity, which is the equivalent of pouring molasses into a gear box. The gears still work, but the speed is reduced, and you can only produce a meager result — not to mention the high likelihood of malfunctioning.

So, if you can't control the environment, circumstances, or context you are in, my best advice is this: control what you can control and take solace in knowing you are doing what you can.

Control your thoughts and choose positivity. Choose the brighter path that will fortify you through the bad times and supercharge you during the good times.

## (12)

# THE BENEFITS, PART 2

*Have you ever wished* that you could do something that would have a profound and positive impact on the world? Me, too. I spent many of the last handful of years ready, willing, and able to "do my part" if only someone showed up on my doorstep to tell me what to do with a guarantee that it would make an actual difference.

When that didn't happen (no matter how much I wished for it), I began my own search for what "everyday people" could do to contribute to the betterment of our world. You are reading the culmination of that initial search, and I intend to continue down this path for the remainder of what I hope is my very long life and report out what I find along the way.

By reading this book, you are already a part of the movement to make a profound and positive impact on the world. I'll confess I do not know what this will look like in five, ten, or fifty years. And that's OK, it is not for me to decide. What I'm responsible for is the intent, and the actions I take in the present moment to support my intent. The same is true for you: don't worry about the ultimate outcome of your efforts to help improve the situation, just keep moving forward with faith that your efforts are a net positive — especially compared to doing nothing at all.

I have seen the power of a positive mindset at my own individual level. Every aspect of my life has improved since I personally adopted the Blueprint to Happy. I believe that while in this positive state my presence has improved the lives of the people around me, too. Mostly because I have been told as much by people like Aunt Ada who inspired me to go on this journey in the first place. As a result, part 2 of the benefits of this Blueprint has become possible — the ability to collectively level up.

## The Benefits, Part 2 of the Blueprint to Happy

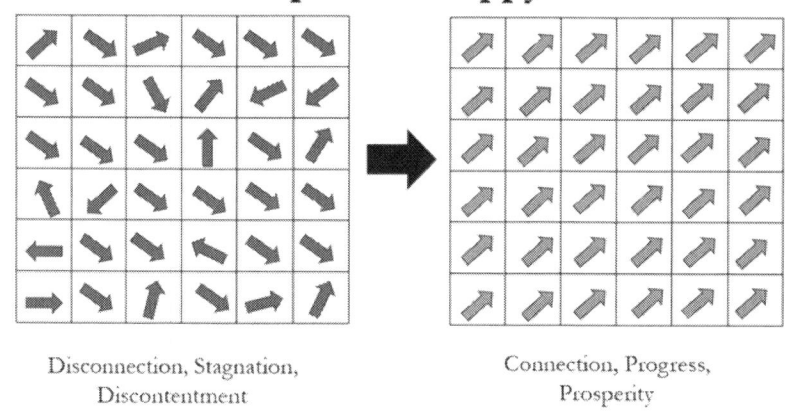

Disconnection, Stagnation, Discontentment

Connection, Progress, Prosperity

Figure 11 – the power of moving in the same direction

Take a look at the diagram above. Imagine each arrow representing an individual. The lefthand side represents our current situation: individuals are disconnected, disjointed, and aimless in their directions. The righthand side represents what it could look like if a common positive mindset was adopted by all, opening up the possibility of moving forward together, aligned and connected.

This is the tipping point I spoke about in the introduction of this book — it doesn't require every arrow to point in the same direction, just a majority of arrows. A tipping point occurs when enough people adopt a practice, and *those* kinetic forces are what take over. Right now, most people have adopted indifference, cynicism, or apathy as their main mode of existing. I don't blame folks for this — it's a tough world out there and without an alternative, removing yourself from the fray is a survival mechanism.

But now the alternative has been laid at your feet. The alternative is to tune in with a positive, actionable, and reality-based perspective. It's a numbers game, and it is also a game of inches. Every little bit of progress, every little bit of telling ourselves a better story, every little bit of helping others feel better about the world and their place in it counts. And the growth, while measured in inches, can be exponential if enough people get on board.

How can this be leveraged to our collective advantage? Let's take a look …

## A POST-FEAR WORLD

There are forces at work that benefit from our negativity bias. Negativity, and fear in particular, is used as a tactic to grab our attention and to ensure we have an emotional reaction so that we will be both receptive to what comes next and will remember it after the moment has passed. By training your brain to prefer positivity, you will build a resistance to this tactic, and if enough people build a resistance, we will be able to break free from a particularly nasty negativity cycle. Think of what a post-fear world could look like in the context of news and politics specifically. What is the purpose of fear in either of these forums? Simply put: to manipulate the audience and electorate.

If you are someone who wishes to make a positive impact in the world, you can do so by being harder to manipulate with negativity. You can help your friends and family by modeling your independence and share with them this Blueprint when they become curious enough to achieve what you have achieved.

Fear is a useful emotion, however, the reasons we become fearful in the modern world are often hypothetical, imaginary, or exaggerated. Being able to determine what is worthy of fear on a day-to-day basis is one of the benefits you can realize through the Blueprint to Happy because you will become better at creating a sense of safety at will. When you feel safe, you are better at assessing the true seriousness of situations.

Even when fear is an appropriate response, it serves your best interests to be able to meet the moment calmly. You can do that for yourself by telling a story about what is happening. For example: "John was in a car accident and he's injured. He's getting care and the immediate danger has passed. I'll pack up some things to take to the hospital and let others know what is happening." Just by going through this narration you are creating a sense of control and focusing on the positive all while acknowledging the situation as it is.

If you are feeling fear, anger, hate, or sadness daily, you should take this as a sign of some major imbalance in your life. Leverage the best practice of minding your mental meals to take an audit of what you are consuming, which will help you determine if your feelings of anxiety are internally driven, or more likely, externally driven.

## THE COMMUNITY HAPPINESS PROJECT

You might recall that I made a confession in the Introduction: while the intent of this book is to help you at an individual level to improve your life, my ultimate goal is to recruit you into what I call the Community Happiness Project (CHP), which becomes easier once you have aligned yourself to the Blueprint.

The Blueprint to Happy is what made the CHP possible. Once I used the Blueprint to lift myself out of the self-inflicted cycle of negativity that was holding me down, I was able to open my mind up to what I was personally capable of doing to make a positive difference in the world. From my place of elevated consciousness, I was able to take stock of what resources I had to help me accomplish my goals. I was able to assess the challenges that exist and ideate on what things I could personally do to move the dial.

Writing has always been a passion of mine, so writing a book seemed like the obvious avenue to actualize my goal of helping others. But I knew I needed something more compelling than a simple theory applied to a single person to demonstrate the power of the message I wanted to deliver. Since positivity was the key to my own personal success and transformation, I decided to direct that focus on my community.

I am fortunate enough to be a property owner, and my lot sits on the corner of one of many small neighborhoods in St. Petersburg, Florida. Before discovering the Blueprint, I had lived in the neighborhood for 10 years and only knew a few of my neighbors. Imagine: this is the place I spend the most time, these are the people who are the physically closest to me, and I barely knew any of them! (Does this sound familiar to you?) The most exposure I'd gotten to the people I shared a street with was in the aftermath of hurricanes, when we'd all wander out and assess the damage. In the case of power outages, we'd run extension cords from neighbors with working power to those without. We would share water and other supplies, and once the crisis had passed, we'd go back to barely interacting.

Thanks to COVID, I was spending a lot more time in my own

neighborhood, biking, walking, and finally observing the changes of the seasons and patterns of the people as they went about their daily lives. I began to notice how much foot traffic happened by my corner lot. The corner, I must confess, was quite barren — little more than a patch of dirt, weeds and dead leaves. In fact, dog walkers would frequently cut across my corner to shorten their walks, because — why not? There wasn't anything there.

Old Adam may have gotten a little perturbed at people cutting through his yard. But New Adam saw this and realized the opportunity to put something interesting and fun on the corner so it would become memorable in a positive way for passing neighbors. This would accomplish the goal of spreading positivity, passive as it might be. I became intrigued by the idea of a signpost with arrows pointing to different places around the world and their respective distances. This concept was very much inspired by my inner child (see best practice: reconnect with your childhood); as a kid, I spent countless hours on my neighborhood streets studying everything from local wildlife (lizards, roly-poly's, snakes, etc.) to cool mailboxes that were replicas of people's houses. I was also obsessed with world maps and globes, so little kid Adam would have been *thrilled* to have a signpost appear in his neighborhood with exotic places all around the world that he could study.

In the city of St. Petersburg and my hometown Gulfport Florida there is a gentleman by the name of Gary King who manufactures and mounts red and yellow signs all around town that simply say "HAPPINESS" as part of what he calls the Happiness Experiment. His theory is that if people see the word HAPPINESS often enough, it will generate actual feelings of happiness and improve the disposition of all who see them. Both St. Petersburg and Gulfport are pretty happy and accepting places, so I think he might be onto something.

Inspired by the Happiness Experiment, I envisioned one of the iconic Happiness Experiment signs topping off the signpost with an accompanying arrow pointing down. The message would be that you can go to many places around the world, near and far, but happiness is right here where you are standing. And once you harness happiness, you can take it with you anywhere you go.

I shared this idea with Aunt Ada, and it stayed an idea until her springtime visit to Florida when she offered to help make the signs over the upcoming summer during my visit to Michigan. This small offering was the first domino to fall — all I needed was a little nudge — and then I was off to the races. A few days later, I noticed my neighbor was putting old blocks at the curb for trash pickup, and asked if I could have them instead. She agreed and helped me haul a dozen or so blocks to my corner to hold the space for the signpost that would not arrive for several months. Not wishing my neighbors to think this heap of blocks was trash, I decided to get creative and made a stone seat out of the blocks just as I might with Legos. On a broken hexagonal paver, I crudely chalked the words, "Coming Soon." This was in March of 2023.

Adam sparks intrigue before breaking ground on the CHP

After that, natural human curiosity took over. Dog walkers would pause and inspect the crude sculpture before moving on. Neighbors driving by would slow down and ask me what was coming soon if they saw me out and about. Once people knew more, they would excitedly share ideas for what could be included in this new project, and every time I talked to someone new, the plans for the spot got better and better.

Eventually, so many inquiries came in that I created a web page to explain what was coming soon and taped a QR code on the block structure that would take them to the page. Through the flood light camera installed over my driveway, I had the privilege of witnessing the beauty of human inquisitiveness as people slowed, and then paused to make sense of what they were seeing. I often wonder what was going through their heads, especially as I continued to iterate on the space.

Curious neighbors check out an early version of the CHP

As spring carried on, I spent weekends looking for ways to add to the corner to make it more interesting. A metal flower that spun with the wind. A basket with laminated cards that shared the same

Best Practices for Happiness as outlined in this book. A bright yellow bench to rest on, a concrete meditating rabbit found on Easter day, which has since become the unofficial mascot of the Community Happiness Project spot. Laminated mission slips encouraging people to complement a stranger or to bust out their favorite dance move. A life-sized dachshund (DASH the dachshund) sculpture complete with collar, leash, and accompanying poop bags as an offering to our local dog walkers. The more engagement I saw with this crude happiness spot, the more excited I became about what it could be. I decided to go all in and make the space as inviting and engaging as possible.

A local business was contracted (who gave me a great deal after hearing about the concept) to install a 15-foot diameter circular pad of AstroTurf — the kind you'd see at playgrounds — to make the space more inviting. The blocks donated by my neighbor were used to make a walking path from the corner to the AstroTurf to make it clear this was a space meant for interaction and engagement. A pair of poles were erected and prayer flags strung between them, along with a little sign that explained the purpose of prayer flags: to spread messages of compassion on the wind each time the flags were taken by a breeze.

The help of my artistic sister was recruited to create what are now known as Happiness Rocks — rocks that are colorfully painted, silly, or inspirational. We put out instructions for neighbors to take a rock and place it somewhere outside their homes where they will see it when they leave and come home. We asked them to pause each time they laid eyes on the rock and think about the things that made them happy recently. Once, while chatting with Aunt Ada through air pods on a trash pickup walk, I spotted a Happiness Rock sitting right at the base of a neighbor's mailbox. This may still go down as one of my happiest moments since beginning the Community Happiness Project — a visual indicator that the CHP was working!

We started the Happiness Rocks because it's a numbers game. This was the goal: to inject more positivity into people's lives so they develop a preference for positivity over time. The rocks were — and are to this day — a big hit. We offer unpainted rocks for people to take and paint at home. Many painted rocks have returned to the Happiness spot to be added to "Monty" the Python, our rock snake inspired by many rock snakes taking social media by storm over this same period.

Bright yellow lounge chairs were added, along with a 15-minute sand timer with a query written on the top and bottom: can you spend 15 minutes being mindful and present? Couples walking have sat facing each other in these chairs, enjoying the space and each other's time. Others have taken up the bench with a book, explaining they lived nearby but didn't have a quiet place to sit like the Happiness spot. When summer came, visiting kids gathered in the spot and played with the bubbles donated by a mystery neighbor, and spun the growing wind decorations or pet DASH the dachshund. Parents stop at the spot in their cars, letting their kids hop out to look for anything new. I once had the pleasure of seeing a young father showing his baby around the CHP in one of those front-facing slings. He paused at anything shiny or colorful and several times — seemingly without thinking about it — kissed the top of his baby's head with fatherly affection. I hope their experience at the CHP is one they will remember for years to come. Fellow neighbors have donated to the spot, each one of them making their own mark on the community space.

Another feature of the Community Happiness Project spot is our "Read a Love Note, Write a Love Note" book. Neighbors are encouraged to interact with each other using small notes about what they are grateful for, and there have been some truly lovely messages conveyed in these pages since the spot has been active. This one is my personal favorite:

> "This brought me out of a dark place. Thanks so much for such a thoughtful and selfless act.
>
> I'm trying to turn my life around. I won't blame the world but you know that feeling you get when nothing is going right and you feel like the world's out to get you?
>
> Places like this are a reminder that **IS NOT TRUE**! There is kindness and wonderful people in this world.
>
> Remember (and I tell this to myself everyday) …
> **Every setback is a setup for a comeback**.
> P.S. – More people should be like this family."
> — G, 26 May 2023

This person was not alone in how they felt about the spot. Here are the thoughts others took the time to share:

> "There is such a kind presence here, and I thank you for that! There are so many things to be grateful for today — the ability to breathe, move, and have our being as a unique spirit in this human experience. Thank you for spreading joy to the neighborhood."
> — A, 9 May 2023

*

> "I am very grateful that I live in a neighborhood where we all look out for one another. Also for God letting me be here after all that I have gone through

these past 2 years. Thank you for putting out this book and letting people know you care." — P, 14 May 2023

*

"I am Love. I give Love. I receive Love. <3 EVERY day I am reminded of this! Thank you for sharing your love and kindness today with me. What a <u>great</u> idea! My heart is full of gratitude and hope. May we all be blessed and create more love and happiness in the world!" — D, 15 May 2023

*

"Good evening. As I visit this corner with my family on a blissful dog walk, we thank you. This is amazing. What you're doing for the community…for us! This neighborhood is lucky to have you a part of it. I grew up right here in the same one. 31 years & counting. And I'm 31! :) Beautiful to see such unity. You made our night." — mom, J, B & D, 16 May 2023

*

"I love this!! It's like stepping back in time, when you could also use honorist boxes — like if you grew fruit you could sell them road side with a box for donations — you must be a very kind hearted person and I thank you for bringing happiness and a quiet place to sit into my neighborhood. God bless you." — 10 Jun 2023

After the rain got the best of our first notebook, we put out another and it wasn't long before this note appeared:

> "It is an honor to be the first to write in this notebook. A community gratitude journal is something that can bring us all together. I am grateful for the equanimity that this space brings. Only come to this spot a few times and it has brought nothing but serenity to my life. Grateful for all the tools this space brings to help me ground myself and connect with my neighborhood. Grateful for my health and also how well this pen writes. Hope to keep coming back. May you get everything you deserve in life." — JR
> 24 Jun 2023

The notes have filled me with joy many times over and affirm that the intent of the Happiness spot is translating into reality.

As the CHP spot has gotten more and more elaborate, a supporting Facebook group was created to increase our reach and hopefully inspire people in communities across the nation to create their own Community Happiness Project spot. Being a project participant requires one simple commitment — that you will make an effort to inject as much positivity into your life as possible. Easy enough, right?

The official mission of the Community Happiness Project is to create happiness through increased positivity in our communities that spreads to the world. The CHP focuses on spaces because visual elements can serve as important reminders that positivity is very real. Think about how your day can be brightened by turning a corner and seeing something unexpectedly delightful — this is the "pop-up" potential of these spaces. Community members can add to spaces like these in little ways and feel like an important part of a larger movement.

The Blueprint to Happy is about the interior work needed to generate happiness within yourself, so that you can take it wherever you go. The Community Happiness Project is about sharing that inner happiness with those closest to you.

The Community Happiness Project is just getting started. We held our official Launch Party on July 2$^{nd}$ of 2023, inviting community members to come out and paint rocks. Dozens of folks joined us, despite a very hot 100° F plus Florida day. The nine-hour day was filled with smiles, words of gratitude, and joy. When it was time to pack up, everyone chipped in without prompting, resulting in a speedy breakdown and a sooner reprieve from the heat for me! It may seem like a small thing, but to me it was just more proof that the Community Happiness Project was working; communities help each other, and that sense of belonging and connectedness is one of the many pathways to happiness.

The Community Happiness Launch Party, July 2nd, 2023

The day after our launch party, I fulfilled a promise I made as part of my Prioritize My Life commitment to spend more quality time with my friends and family — especially the ones that lived far away. I packed up my car and embarked on a two-month-long working road trip. Not only would I get to spend weeks at a time with far-away family, I would also get to work on the construction of the center piece of the Community Happiness Project. It is still incredible to think about how so much joy and positivity was brought to the community even before the signpost was erected! My road trip took me to five states, visiting friends and family all while maintaining my day-job thanks to the work-from-anywhere capabilities brought to us via COVID necessity.

The road trip was filled with wonderful new experiences, and the opportunity to deepen relationships with family I was already close with, as well as begin the process of getting to know my extended family better. I delivered customized Happiness Rocks painted by my sister along the way, and with the help of my aunt and uncle, designed, cut, sanded, painted, and sealed the colorful signs that would be the central part of the Community Happiness Project spot. With signs in hand, they came with me for the rest of my trip, where I had my family sign their favorites so that they, too, could be a part of the project.

In the quiet twilight of Northern Michigan while staying with my mom and uncle, I finished the first draft of this book and printed it for my biggest fan (mom, of course!) to have the first full read. She and the wonderful and lovely beta readers who have agreed to read the early version of this work have all reported great outcomes in applying the Blueprint to their lives and have shared helpful insights that has allowed me to make this book even better for readers of the final publication.

I returned home from my summer road trip on September 6th,

and with the help of my dad and sister, the signpost was standing tall at the center of the Community Happiness Project spot on September 9th, 2023. The final product exceeded even my greatest expectations, and it is hard to accurately describe the feelings of joy and satisfaction of taking something that started as a wild idea and turning into a tangible reality. What was even better was sharing the journey with every single person who supplied support, materials, ideas, physical labor, and encouragement to keep the dream alive.

Upon my return, I was faced with an unexpected opportunity to apply the Blueprint by way of a cat named Lucy — the same one who often accompanied me on my trash pickup walks. It turns out Lucy was embarking on her own personal happiness journey, too. Eleven years prior, this orange, black, and white calico cat made her appearance on my doorstep. She was both friendly and adorable, and seemed to think the house I had recently purchased was also her house. It didn't take long for her to wear down my resolve, and soon enough I was undergoing the process of figuring out what kind of food she liked. A few months in, her belly grew suspiciously large, and five kittens later I formally adopted her through a local program called Friends of Strays. The program was able to find homes for her kittens (not hard, they were adorable like her), and a cat now *formally* named Lucy would be my companion for the next decade.

Lucy living the Good Life

Lucy was a blessing from the day she arrived at my house, keeping me company and cuddling close when I was sick or generally not feeling well. She was a calm and grounding presence with striking yellow eyes that loved watching squirrels and birds from my office picture window. Having grown up on the streets, she was not a cat that could be kept indoors indefinitely. In addition to general cat adventures, she enjoyed visiting with other houses, to the extent that when my next-door neighbor and I replaced our adjoining fence, they had a cat door installed so that Lucy could more easily drop by for visits. She amused locals by following me when I walked to the store, patrolled around the neighborhood picking up litter, or visited Little Free Libraries.

For a long time, it was just Lucy and me, until 2022 when another feline — a black and white tuxedo cat we call Bruce — showed up and used the Lucy Playbook to gain residence at our house (minus the kittens). This development was tolerable but not ideal for Lucy, and the last straw for her seemed to be my extra-long road trip, which was probably closer to a year rather than two months in cat time.

I know because upon my return from my road trip, I learned that Lucy was coming home less and less. Instead, she had found a new house to take up residence. The existing occupants took her to Friends of Strays, who contacted me to see if my cat was missing.

It turns out she wasn't missing, so much as she had rehomed herself! Just one block away, to a house with a lovely screened-in porch surrounded by greenery and perhaps most importantly for Lucy … no other cats.

In chatting with my newfound neighbors, I found that they were enjoying Lucy's company very much and did not mind if she stuck around. They were willing to look after her and made sure she had food and water. Because Lucy had found me, and not the other way around, I felt like it was ultimately up to her where she lived. Even still, my feelings about this new development were complicated. I missed Lucy's companionship while I was on my road trip, and I was looking forward to long restful hours with her curled up beside me. I could barely wait to hand out ear scritches and to feel her happy purring again. I thought about all the other times I had returned from trips and how I would barely be able to move because she would take up residence on my lap for the first several hours of returning.

So, when I traversed the block to my neighbor's house, I was thrilled when Lucy easily recognized me and followed me home, meowing excitedly the whole time. We visited, but somehow it wasn't the same. Soon enough she wanted to go back outside so that she could return to her quiet screened-in porch. The next time making the trek, I had to encourage her to follow me, and then on the third time, I walked home with Lucy contently watching me go from her new front yard.

My initial reaction to this development was disappointment and sadness, but thanks to the Blueprint, I was able to notice what was happening. Over the space of a few days, possibly a week, I gave myself time to consider the situation. The most important factor to me was Lucy's safety and happiness, both of which were very well established at her new home. Another factor was how much upcoming travel I had planned. I had always felt a little guilty about leaving Lucy for long periods of time, knowing she would become stressed and sometimes even get sick if I was gone for too long. Lucy relocating had alleviated some of the guilt I was feeling about the travel I had planned, and all the travel I still wanted to do.

Finally, I told myself the better story: Lucy's getting up in age and deserves a safe and comfortable place to relax as an old lady.

And so, I can imagine that she has gone to a quiet and peaceful retirement home, which is still very accessible for visits. I have even begun to develop an interesting and enriching relationship with what I think of as her new stepparents, and my newfound neighbors. Instead of feeling upset and disappointed, I am happy that she found a solution to both our problems and helped me find new friends. Finally, I put her new residence onto my afternoon neighborhood walking route so that we still cross paths. Sometimes, she sees and follows me home for a visit before heading back to her retirement home.

Lucy visiting the CHP

This is the Blueprint to Happy at work.

I share all of this and the story of the Community Happiness Project with you to demonstrate the profound power of applied positive mindsets. I went from being isolated and unhappy to being connected and joyful with the help of the mindset shift I have outlined for you in this book. Not only have I achieved personal fulfillment, but this new mindset has also created the space in my head and heart to help others in a way that is real, powerful, and very much needed.

This is the story of *one* person deciding to make a change.

From one person, an entire community is seeing a positive change.

Now imagine if that one person turned into ten, and then a hundred, and then five hundred. The possibilities are profound, and you can help realize them.

*We* can help realize them together.

*We* can be part of the solution.

The Community Happiness Project centerpiece

**PRACTICAL APPLICATION #12**

Take a few minutes to jot down notes on the kind of things you might be able to do at a local level that would generate more positivity in your immediate surroundings. Even if you don't feel like you have the time or energy to do these things now, what *would* you want to do if you did have the time and energy?

Get creative, and do not let limitations stop something from making the list. Let your imagination run free. Keep the list and be open to opportunities that arise that could make it a reality. Share your list with your friends and family, as they might be excited to help you make it a reality just as my family was eager to help me.

# (13)

# PARTING WORDS

*How many times* over the course of reading this book did you experience skepticism? Perhaps you found yourself scoffing at the idea that positive thoughts could have any real impact on your life or the world at large. Maybe you felt a physical resistance to the idea of even *trying* to shift your thought patterns. All of these responses are common. I have noticed people have a tendency to want to cling to their current state of being, even if it is not serving them. I've listened to people (including myself!) defend their misery, speaking about it as if there could not possibly be any alternative, and to think otherwise would be naive and out of touch with reality.

I have had people who seem quite unhappy tell me with conviction that they are "happy enough" even as they spend most of their time complaining and going in circles around their stated goals or desires.

In these instances, I recognize the limits of my control and happily continue down my path of positive thinking. I find peace in the idea that my ability to walk the walk may be enough to influence people into following a similar path.

No one can make the choice to improve your life but you. My goal in writing this book is twofold: (1) to raise your level of awareness about the connection between positive mindsets and happiness and (2) to give you a powerful tool to achieve happiness if you make the critical decision to improve not just your life, but the lives of people around you. If you have read this far, I feel confident that I have accomplished my first goal. Beyond that, I accept that the rest is up to you and wish you much luck in whichever path you choose.

If you are still feeling skeptical, allow me to leave you with these final considerations. What is the downside of thinking positively as this book outlines? You are not being asked to deny reality in favor of some imaginary world where everything is perfect. Perhaps the idea of self-examining as required in the Investigation step is daunting or difficult. In this case, it may be a helpful step for you to seek out a therapist who can help you self-discover in a safe and nonjudgmental space. Maybe you are afraid of trying because you might fail and feel like a failure as a result. This is a fear response, and perhaps your first task should be using the Blueprint to unpack this fear of failure and tell yourself a better story.

Something like … "Anytime I try something new it will take some time to get the hang of. This is an investment in myself, and I'm worth investing in. Any attempt to improve my life is time well spent!"

Much of this book has been written over the summer of 2023, three years after a global pandemic rocked the world and had many of us sheltering in place. This is the first year that travel resembles something close to "normal" for many, and the first year I decided to take the peace of mind I have recently come to know and do something with it. In this case, it was deciding to take a two-month-long working road trip to visit family and friends after a very long hiatus.

And not just long because of COVID — long because I hadn't been prioritizing friends or family much before the pandemic. I had fallen into the delayed happiness fallacy. I would visit my family when … I would enjoy time away when … I would explore new locations when … Always sometime off in the indeterminate future. And then I did the math.

One of the stops along my way was to spend three weeks with my mom and her side of the family in a small town called Munising, Michigan. It is a place I have been to before, both when I was very young and as an adult. I used to describe it as a "Small one-streetlight town. And the one streetlight is a flasher."

A point of fact: the streetlight has since been replaced with a roundabout, which is far superior to a streetlight.

Since returning to Munising in my new state of mind — peace and happiness — I have come to realize just how much I overlooked about this beautiful place because I was too busy being in my head, making judgements, and feeding the default negativity that lived inside of me. Now when I look around, all I see is beauty and serenity. Quaint shops, friendly locals, abundant wildlife, endless trails, and adventure around every corner. All these things were here each time I had visited in the past, but I was incapable of seeing them thanks to my negativity bias. I can look back now with clear vision and see how unresponsive I was to the wonders that surrounded me, and I find myself grateful that is no longer the case.

In how many ways might this be true for you in your own life?

Think about what might still be out there, literally right around the corner if only you could see and appreciate it.

I am a writer of many years and I still find it difficult to fully describe the transformation that becomes possible when you embrace positivity as a preference. I am left to simply appeal to you to embrace the Blueprint to Happy and experience it for yourself to understand the full glory of what positivity has to offer.

What future awaits you?

# (13.1)

# YOU'RE DONE READING! NOW WHAT?

*Congratulations on finishing* the Blueprint to Happy! So, what should you do now that you've gotten this far? Here are eight things you can do to set yourself up for success with your new knowledge:

1. Get some **quality sleep**. Your brain stores information into long term memory overnight, and you definitely want this Blueprint around for future reference.
2. Practice the process **at your own pace** — give yourself grace when it is called for and **re-read these chapters** as many times as is useful.
3. Make time to regularly practice the **three to five Best Practices** that resonated with you the most.

4. **Upgrade your response** to "how are you?" when people ask (Fantastic! Wonderful! Amazing!) and notice their response.
5. **Adopt a mantra or maxim** that helps keep you on track where you know you might have a hard time doing so.
6. Be sure to **return for the three and six month** Positive and Negative Emotion Inventory **assessment** to check your progress.
7. **Share** this book with your family and friends!
8. Think more people should read the Blueprint? Consider leaving a **Review** for this book on Amazon or Goodreads so that others can join you on this journey.

---

Scan the QR code below to watch a feature of the Community Happiness Project on 10 Tampa Bay News' Beautiful People special segment.

# (14)

# REFERENCES

*In addition to my personal experience* and experimentation with the concepts laid out in this book, what you have read was made possible thanks to the many great resources available to help those who are willing to learn and grow. In other words, I am not only the author of personal development non-fiction, I am also the consummate consumer of them.

Below you will find the most influential books to my own personal development. Over the years, I have developed a talent for connecting the dots across topics and learnings that may not seem related at first. My ability to summarize these connected learnings in a succinct and useful way is the reason the Blueprint to Happy exists. If you want to take a deep dive into those connections, this list is the perfect place to start.

- → *NLP: The Essential Guide to Neuro-Linguistic Programming* by Tom Hoobyar
- → *Positivity: Groundbreaking Research Reveals How to Embrace the Hidden Strength of Positive Emotions, Overcome Negativity, and Thrive* by Barabara Fredrickson, Ph. D

- *A Culture of Happiness: How to Scale Up Happiness from People to Organizations* by Tho Ha Vinh, Ph. D
- *The Tools: 5 Tools to Help You Find Courage, Creativity, and Willpower – and Inspire You To Live Life in Forward Motion* by Phil Stutz and Barry Michels
- *Meditations* by Marcus Aurelius
- *How to Stop Worrying and Start Living* by Dale Carnagie
- *What Happened to You* by Bruce Perry, M.D. Ph. D and Oprah Winfrey
- *No Bad Parts* by Richard Schwartz
- *The Body Keeps the Score* by Bessel Van Der Kolk
- *The Nazis Knew My Name: A Remarkable Story of Survival and Courage in Auschwitz-Birkenau* by Magda Hellinger
- *Man's Search for Meaning* by Viktor Frankl

# ABOUT THE AUTHOR

*Adam Deters,* a native Floridian with family ties to Michigan, grew up in Gulfport before settling in St. Petersburg. He pursued his education at the University of South Florida St. Petersburg, where he graduated with a degree in political science — a choice that emerged as a compromise between his initial interests in business and history. In the realm of political science, Adam delved into the intricacies of human behavior, empirical statistics, and research methodologies, refining his approach to learning and communication.

Graduating in 2009, his early career opportunities paved the way for his eventual specialization as a process and change management expert. Adam's extensive experience across diverse business sectors has shaped his communication style, characterized by its accessibility and his analytical acumen. This unique blend enables him to distill advanced psychological concepts into simple processes, empowering others to navigate successfully toward happiness even in challenging circumstances.

This passion for connecting dots serves as his driving force, evident in his commitment to sharing his insights with the world through his passion project — the Blueprint. Through the Blueprint and the sharing of his personal journey, Adam hopes to inspire readers to connect their own dots, embark on a journey of learning, and experience personal growth that enriches their lives with the things that they love.

Made in the USA
Columbia, SC
26 April 2024